SHE IS
Uncompromising

www.amplifypublishing.com

She Is Uncompromising: A Christian Woman's Guide to Mastering Motherhood, Business, and Everything in Between

For more information, please contact:
Amplify, an imprint of Amplify Publishing Group
620 Herndon Parkway, Suite 320
Herndon, VA 20170
info@amplifypublishing.com

Library of Congress Control Number: 2022904686

CPSIA Code: PRV0622A

ISBN-13: 978-1-64543-966-0

Printed in the United States

This book is dedicated to my loving husband, BJ. Thank you for your unwavering support, consistent patience, and unconditional love. I'll never know what I did to deserve you, but I thank God for you every day.

This book is also dedicated to my son. You are my daily reminder that God loves me and hears my prayers. The joy you bring me every day is indescribable. I love you.

SHE IS
Uncompromising

A Christian Woman's Guide

to Mastering Motherhood,

Business, and Everything in Between

TATUM TEMIA AYOMIKE
CEO of Anchored Media

CONTENTS

FOREWORD

SHE IS UNCOMPROMISING IS AN ACCOUNT of observations made by Tatum Temia amidst her growth as a wife, in motherhood, and as a corporate leader. As she looks back at past encounters, Tatum combines scriptures to shine a light on breakthroughs and redemption that could only represent the manifestations of trusting God in seemingly bleak times. Within these pages, the Word of God is brought to life, showing how shifts in focus can and will lead you to answers you never knew existed. Such shifts include setting pride and ego aside, submitting to God's authority, exercising faith, and relying on prayer. She shares intimate details of steering through challenges, coupled with a practical approach to seeking and receiving your desires directly from the Lord. The storytelling and teaching style of this book will undoubtedly inspire and equip you with life-changing yet easily applied methods to claim it all. In an infectious way, you will learn to expect only the best.

I personally have never met another person with the level of passion for their occupation outside of my wife, Tatum

Temia. Her work gives her so much joy that she can practically eat, sleep, and breathe it due to the satisfaction that comes from her efforts. I've also never met anyone with the kind of hyperfocus she has. I've seen her "in the zone," sorting through ideas so intentionally that she unintentionally drowns out the noise and conversations that could be happening around her. She devotes 100 percent to the quality of her craft, taking no shortcuts.

Tatum's investments in learning and development have raised her understanding, diversified her perspectives, and opened the door for her to continuously add value to everyone with whom she works. Any useful piece of information she's gained over time is carefully woven into her products and services, providing clients with advantageous resources. Tatum demonstrates a pure, rare love for clients, colleagues, close friends, and family. She is an encouraging, empowering influence who leads so many others to transform and conquer life's unique challenges. She has had this effect on me in my own journey to master my field of public accounting, as she embodies the distinction and excellence found through studying God's Word. Her work teaches others to be faithful and to seek God's Kingdom in pursuit of the life they truly desire. She is able to ascend in business while making a happy, healthy home for our family. Her mission, which she views as a personal duty, is extremely important, leading her to approach every project with a plan and close attention to small details. This book is another product crafted with her careful approach.

Tatum breaks down all barriers between her and her goals. She does not settle for compliments and external praise, due to her natural internal drive to outdo her last output. Her main motivation is to be pleasing to God. Tatum is human, and (like all of us) she experiences that inner struggle against the number-one enemy—herself. What is remarkable for me is that I am able to witness, firsthand, Tatum's uncanny ability to walk in victory over herself. Like many others, I aspire to consistently win the battle against myself, and here in *She Is Uncompromising*, she provides loads of knowledge on how we can gain resolve through our relationship with God. Tatum's first book, *Blessed + Bossed Up*, told the profound story of growing pains in a season of discovery in which God was not only a partner but the leader of all her endeavors. In contrast, *She Is Uncompromising* describes how you can balance it all while winning the fight.

BAWO AYOMIKE, CPA

INTRODUCTION

"How do you feel about all you have to sacrifice for yourself in order to be a wife and a mother?"

I was asked this question as I was making small talk with a client prior to our meeting. This question really struck a chord with me because it is laced with the assumption that I do have to sacrifice myself to be a wife and a mother and somehow I must deal emotionally with that on a day-to-day basis. The question wasn't asked with any negative connotation, but the way it was presented showed me that the person asking didn't even consider that it is possible to not have to sacrifice myself to excel in my family life. I ended up asking a follow-up question inquiring why they assumed I was sacrificing something, because it was obvious from our working relationship that I had things going on outside of being a wife and mom. She told me that she always heard about women discussing what they'd given up in order to have a family, and it made her question if she wanted to get married and have children altogether; she couldn't imagine a life not living up to her full potential. This made me wonder how many women have incorrectly assumed the same. Who made this rule that, as a woman, your goals, dreams, and big ideas are the sacrificial lamb for a thriving marriage and children? It certainly wasn't God. If I can do all things through Christ who strengthens me (Philippians 4:13), does that only apply to my roles where I serve my household?

I had an identity before I said "I do" and before I gave birth to my son. I had a destiny to fulfill on Earth before I was formed in my mother's womb (Jeremiah 1:5). But even in the world of online entrepreneurship, I find myself torn. There's a space where there are many achieving women who have successful companies, influence, and lavish lifestyles full of adventure and delight. They thrive in their professional settings, and it shows in all that they've been able to accomplish. I admire these women and can relate to what they have accomplished and how they're striving for more. But the relatability comes to an abrupt halt when I learn of the time and personal energy they are putting into their companies on a daily basis. As a woman who has always desired to have a family of my own, I knew this type of work schedule would not translate to me maintaining a happy home. So though there is a season for everything under Heaven (Ecclesiastes 3), I needed business strategies that would be transferable to when my life no longer allows me to spend days at a time behind my computer screen and constantly connected with what's going on in the business world.

On the other hand, there are women who have dedicated themselves to their families. They have beautiful homes and cook every meal from scratch, and the affairs of their family are perfectly timed to the minute. I admire these women as well. They create joyful and efficient homes that anyone would be pleased to come home to. They take joy in seeing their household thrive, and it's a role that is not given enough credit. These women often have wonderful blogs, YouTube channels, and other brands, which they're able to monetize, and they build successful businesses around their abilities. I desire for my home to be a place of joy with managerial precision. I enjoy making meals from scratch for my family, blending my son's baby food, and having the perfect holiday photos in which not a hair is misplaced. But once again, the relatability comes to a halt. Being a homemaker is a full-time job that should never be undermined or underestimated. However, I can't give that much time to maintaining my household to that level while also building a company that isn't centered around my family (which requires full-time hours and effort). It will leave me burnt out and no good for either. It is my desire to do both—is it realistic? My answer: Absolutely. I refuse to believe otherwise.

I read once that strongholds are created when we as believers accept a thought/idea/lifestyle/emotion that is contrary to the Word of God. This stronghold gives a safe space for the enemy to hide and continue his plan to kill, steal, and destroy (John 10:10) while being completely anonymous. And in that safe space, he can keep you from God's best without you even knowing it's him, because you've unconsciously accepted a lie as truth. When you accept the idea that you have to sacrifice yourself or your ambition for your family, a stronghold is created that will lead you to one of two things: 1) Burying your dreams and desires completely, or

2) Throwing yourself into work and fulfillment and never starting a family in the first place. This can also look like starting a family, but the marriage ends in divorce because the household was neglected for the career. While they are two different paths, they both lead to the same place: settling.

I personally do not believe that as women we have to settle in any area of our lives. We can have it all: the family, the business, the ministry, the influence, the affluence, and the wealth. Whatever our hearts desire, we can have—as long as we delight ourselves in the Lord (Psalm 37:4). And because God said He can do exceedingly and abundantly above anything we can ask for or think (Ephesians 3:20), we can have even more than that. The only question left is how, and that's what we are going to focus on in this book. We are dismantling the lie that we have to shrink to fit into the box that society has created for women. If, as believers, rivers of living water are going to flow through us (John 7:38), we were never meant to fit in a box in the first place. What's inside us is too powerful to be contained.

Over the course of this book, we are going to cover very specific elements of who we are as women that often keep us from fully embodying all that God has called us to be, without settling in any area. It's important to note that this book isn't just for the woman who is already married with children, looking to balance it all. Rather, this book is for any woman who refuses to settle. This book is for the woman who may wear many hats but desires to sport them all with grace, class, and efficiency. This book is for the uncompromising.

Let's get to work . . .

CHAPTER 1

WHAT IT MEANS TO COMPROMISE

com·pro·mise

/ˈkämprəˌmīz/ **noun**

an agreement or a settlement of a dispute that is reached by each side making concessions.

In order to truly get to an uncompromising place, we can't skip over what compromise is and how it comes about. We also can't water down how powerful it is and how detrimental it can be to our total life success. Compromise isn't necessarily a "heavy" word, and it can be used constructively in certain contexts. For example, if you're having a dispute with your husband, it would be productive to offer concessions in some way in order to come to an understanding. Being uncompromising in this sense would avoid any prolonged conflict. Even in business, when you are negotiating a deal, the sweet spot usually happens when both parties give a little to reach a mutual agreement. Since compromise has its place in certain scenarios, it isn't always considered in the way it can be: a self-sabotaging behavior keeping women all over the world settling for a life less than they want and less than what God has for them. That's why we have to start here. Just because compromise has its appropriate place, it doesn't mean that it needs to be a consistent theme in our lives.

Let's analyze compromise and how it can be a silent success killer, when underestimated:

2 Corinthians 10:4–6: New Living Translation

We use God's mighty weapons, not worldly weapons, to knock down the strongholds of human reasoning and to destroy false arguments. We destroy every proud obstacle that keeps people from knowing God. We capture their rebellious thoughts and teach them to obey Christ. And after you have become fully obedient, we will punish everyone who remains disobedient.

Stronghold is a war term, and in its simplest definition means a fortified place that is well protected against attack. An interesting definition I came across defined a stronghold as a place dominated by a certain group or belief system. In my research, I have discovered that a stronghold can be fortified one of two ways:

In God/His Word (they're one), or 2) Human reasoning/world systems. One generates freedom, the other produces bondage.

In the Bible, God is referenced as a stronghold:

Isaiah 25:4 (Amplified Bible): For You have been a stronghold for the helpless, a stronghold for the poor in his distress, a shelter from the storm, a shade from the heat; For the breath of tyrants is like a rainstorm against a wall.

Psalm 9:9 (New International Version): The Lord also will be a refuge and a stronghold for the oppressed, a refuge in times of trouble.

Psalm 46:7 (Amplified Bible): The Lord of hosts is with us; The God of Jacob is our stronghold [our refuge, our high tower]. Selah

Proverbs 10:29 (New Living Translation): The way of the Lord is a stronghold to those with integrity, but it destroys the wicked.

A stronghold secured by the Lord is the ultimate protection. It's a safe sanctuary that provides shelter, power, and redemption. When a stronghold is reinforced by human reasoning and world systems, it becomes a crippling structure that creates deep-rooted bondage. Though a stronghold at its core is supposed to be a representation of the protection of God, it becomes bondage when a believer agrees with reasoning and belief systems that are opposite to the Word of God. The fortress that is meant to protect creates an obstruction between you, what God is trying to do through you, and what He is trying to be *to* you.

To properly distinguish between the two manifestations of strongholds, I will refer to human reasoning as a stronghold of bondage. The specific stronghold of bondage we are uprooting in this book is compromise. When you agree with a worldview that you have to settle in any area of your life, you are agreeing with a belief system that is not anchored in truth. This gives the enemy legal access to hide behind the bondage created and advance their plan to destroy you and everything God wants to do through you.

Before we get into the deeper content of this book, I want to ask you this question: Are you fortified in the Word or in the systems of the world? Before we can discuss being uncompromising, you must have the attitude, a settled way of thinking, that God will be your stronghold on this journey. That His Word will be a lamp to your feet and a light on your path. That the desires of your heart are possible and attainable, and that He wants you to have them all. You must be committed to the journey He wants you to take, even if it's uncomfortable and unconventional.

Can you think of a time when you compromised in your life? I can. I can actually name plenty. One that rings loud is how I initially compromised for the American Dream instead of my dream. At a young age, my parents and teachers would always ask, "What do you want to be when you grow up?" I would give answers that varied from a ballerina or a firefighter to a teacher; whatever my young mind could think of that seemed interesting enough. It's amusing to me how, when we're young, we are given the freedom to dream and imagine what we want to be when we grow up. But when we're actually on the cusp of growing up, that freedom becomes a lot more restrained. In high school, I stopped getting asked what I wanted to be when I grew up, and instead, I got groomed on what I needed to do to get into college and fit what I wanted to be into the confines of the American Dream. The narrative of the American Dream is that you get an education in the form of a degree from a university, graduate, get a job in the field you studied, work for more than forty years, retire, and then live your best life during your retirement years. I never saw following this path as a compromise, because I believed that it was what I was supposed to do.

The American Dream became such a stronghold that I got into crazy debt completing my undergraduate degree, added more debt with my graduate degree, and couldn't find a job within my field to save my life. Then once I did, I hated it. At work I had to conform to corporate cultures, which as an African American woman meant fitting into a box that wasn't built for me in the first place. The American Dream was a nightmare; it became a stronghold because I had accepted that it was my path to success and never ever considered another way. When I finally followed my dream, I started a business with no debt—making more in a quarter than I did in a year in corporate America—that impacted millions of people all over the world. And I was able to be 100 percent myself in the process. I'm living my best life right now. That's what being uncompromising ultimately leads to: freedom.

THE THREE DANGERS OF COMPROMISING

1. COMPROMISE INHIBITS OUR TESTIMONY

Genesis 19:14—New International Version

So Lot went out and spoke to his sons-in-law, who were pledged to marry his daughters. He said, "Hurry and get out of this place, because the Lord is about to destroy the city!" But his sons-in-law thought he was joking.

In the Bible, Lot was the type of guy who had a "go-with-the-flow" attitude and behavior. He was a drifter and not one to be intentional and strategic with his decisions. This element of his character caused him to blend in heavily with the sinful behaviors of the culture around him. In Genesis, we learn of the story of Sodom and Gomorrah being destroyed. God had mercy on Lot and his family, giving them an opportunity to escape prior to the destruction. Lot went to deliver the message to his sons-in-law, telling them to leave because the Lord is about to destroy the city. The sons-in-law took what he was saying as a joke and didn't believe him. I believe that Lot compromising his righteousness with his go-with-the-flow nature made his urgent, truthful message questionable. Compromise, in any capacity, discredits the message that God wants to convey through us. In this instance, it was life-or-death, and the unbelievability of Lot's testimony at that time could have cost his family their lives.

A testimony is a powerful tool for the Kingdom of God because it makes what's written in the Word real and believable to people. From a business standpoint, our testimony is equivalent to results-based marketing. It makes it that much easier for a consumer to make a confident buying decision when they can see that whatever is being presented to them works. When we compromise, we hinder the completion of God's plan, which then taints the testimony that we were supposed to have and share with others.

What's particularly interesting about Lot's story is that it wasn't a compromise he made in the moment that caused his sons-in-law to take his message as a joke. When God gave him a chance to spare himself and his family, he jumped on it immediately and went to warn them. But it was the consistent compromising of his lifestyle that discredited him to others. He blended in so well with sin, that it wasn't believable when he was being used by God.

2. COMPROMISE CAUSES US TO NEGOTIATE DIVINE DETAILS

Exodus 8:25–29—New International Version

Then Pharaoh summoned Moses and Aaron and said, "Go, sacrifice to your God here in the land." But Moses said, "That would not be right. The sacrifices we offer the Lord our God would be detestable to the Egyptians. And if we offer sacrifices that are detestable in their eyes, will they not stone us? We must take a three-day journey into *the wilderness to offer sacrifices to the Lord our God, **as he commands us**.*" Pharaoh said, "I will let you go to offer sacrifices to the Lord your God in the wilderness, but you must not go very far. Now pray for me." Moses answered, "As soon as I leave you, I will pray to the Lord, and tomorrow the flies will leave Pharaoh and his officials and his people. Only let Pharaoh be sure that he does not act deceitfully again by not letting the people go to offer sacrifices to the Lord."*

Moses is one of the most popular prophets and an excellent example of leadership. In the preceding passage, a plague of flies came over Pharaoh because of his commitment to keeping the people of Israel in bondage. Desperate to get rid of the affliction, he told Moses and Aaron to go and pray to God to remove the torment. The key moment here is that Pharaoh wanted to dictate how Moses and Aaron prayed. Moses was uncompromising about the details of God's instruction and the specifics of His divine methodology. I wonder—if Moses compromised and gave half-measured obedience, what would that have meant for the Exodus? What would that have meant for you and me? Would the people still be in bondage? Would we?

Compromises often take the form of partial obedience or trying to negotiate with God about the details of His instructions. In several instances, this is encouraged by outside people who want the benefits of God's power but want it to happen in a way that's comfortable to them. Obedience cannot be fragmented.

3. COMPROMISE CAUSES US TO RELAX OUR STANDARDS

As Christians, we are to live righteous lives. With that, there are biblical principles and standards that we must adhere to. Some overlap with common decency, but others conflict with what the world may deem to be widely acceptable. This is why we must be unwavering in our lifestyle, because the moment we relax our standards, we begin to introduce compromise. There are four main doors that present an opportunity for our standards to be relaxed: culture, relationships, pressure, and inconsistency.

CULTURE

Daniel was a prophet who was taken captive and deported to Babylon by Nebuchadnezzar. Nebuchadnezzar was the leader of Babylon and was widely feared. Whenever he invaded a country, he would take the most talented and favorable people back to Babylon. Daniel and his friends fell into these categories. Nebuchadnezzar implemented various tactics to acclimate Daniel and his friends to the Babylonian culture. He introduced them to their education in an attempt to convert their reasoning, and he attempted to convert their lifestyle by changing their diets. He also sought to convert their allegiance by changing their names. Daniel means "God is my judge" in Hebrew, and it was changed to Belteshazzar, which means "Bel protects his life." Bel was the chief Babylonian god. The same was done for Daniel's friends Hananiah

(Shadrach), Mishael (Meshach), and Azariah (Abednego).

This attempted conversion came to a pivotal point, when he and his friends entered into training for the king's service.

Daniel 1:8–16—New International Version

But Daniel resolved not to defile himself with the royal food and wine, and he asked the chief official for permission not to defile himself this way. Now God had caused the official to show favor and compassion to Daniel, but the official told Daniel, "I am afraid of my lord the king, who has assigned your food and drink. Why should he see you looking worse than the other young men your age? The king would then have my head because of you." Daniel then said to the guard whom the chief official had appointed over Daniel, Hananiah, Mishael, and Azariah, "Please test your servants for ten days: Give us nothing but vegetables to eat and water to drink. Then compare our appearance with that of the young men who eat the royal food, and treat your servants in accordance with what you see." So he agreed to this and tested them for ten days. At the end of the ten days they looked healthier and better nourished than any of the young men who ate the royal food. So the guard took away their choice food and the wine they were to drink and gave them vegetables instead.

It's important to note that Daniel's request to continue his particular diet could have gotten all of them killed. It was bold and dangerous for him to try to negotiate with the king.

But Daniel refused to relax his standards and was willing to die if that meant maintaining his commitment to God. Because of his stance, God granted Daniel favor with the official and ultimately spared everyone's life. Daniel adjusted to the culture, but once the adjustments directly opposed his commitment to God, he took a stand and thought quickly on his feet. It worked in his favor.

There are many people in the African American community who do not subscribe to the Christian faith because, historically, our people were enslaved and oppressed using the same Bible that I am quoting in this book. Even today, many conservatives use the Bible to perpetuate hate, racism, and white supremacy. Understandably, many African Americans have decided to seek out their African roots and subscribe to those cultures and spiritual practices. Many of those spiritual practices include the worship of other gods, witchcraft, voodoo, and other things that are condemned in the Christian faith.

As a Black woman, I also desire to know and understand my African heritage. My husband is from the Itsekiri tribe in Nigeria, and I have always admired his knowledge and understanding of where he's from. I appreciate that he knows the language, the food, the music, and the history. He has a level of identity and self-awareness that I wish I had. I have no sense of identity prior to the transatlantic slave trade that brought my ancestors to South Carolina. This is the truth for many African American people, and that's why getting in tune with our African culture is so important. However, the reality is that many of our cultures also include spiritual practices that conflict with the Christian faith. As I seek out my culture, I have to also reject the aspects that don't align with the Word of God, because my ultimate identity is in Him.

Many of us are born into cultures in which we have to adapt in some way, but we must keep in mind to never allow adapting to lead to compromise.

RELATIONSHIPS

2 Corinthians 6:14–18—The Message

Don't become partners with those who reject God. How can you make a partnership out of right and wrong? That's not partnership; that's war. Is light best friends with dark? Does Christ go strolling with the Devil? Do trust and mistrust hold hands? Who would think of setting up pagan idols in God's holy Temple? But that is exactly what we are, each of us a temple in whom God lives. God himself put it this way:

"I'll live in them, move into them;
I'll be their God and they'll be my people.
So leave the corruption and compromise;
leave it for good," says God.
"Don't link up with those who will pollute you.
I want you all for myself.
I'll be a Father to you;
you'll be sons and daughters to me."
The Word of the Master, God.

Relationships can lead to compromise when they require your loyalty to be divided. It's important to analyze if your obligations to a relationship, be it personal or professional, will cause you to relax your standards in any way. With women, this form of compromise often manifests itself in our dating life. Someone once told me that the most important decision you will ever make for your destiny is who you marry. I couldn't agree with this more. Prior to my relationship with my husband, I was in a relationship that checked all of my boxes. He was tall, dark, handsome, enterprising, and Christian. Anything I could have written down, he was, except for one detail. Even though he was a Christian, he was not of the same belief system as me. The denomination or subgroup of Christianity that he identified with and grew up practicing has core differences in their belief system that conflicted with mine. There was a time in which I was so deeply in love that I tried to convince myself that this would be okay. I began looking up interfaith marriages on the Internet because I was trying to rationalize within myself that this could work.

I remember talking to my grandmother about it, and she told me something that I held close to my heart. She said, "Baby, you can't marry a man you can't worship with. How will your family have a foundation when you and your husband are planted in two different soils?" I presented some arguments to her. But, in my heart, I knew she was right. The relationship eventually ended, but my commitment to never compromise because of my emotions is a lesson that I never want to forget. Looking at my marriage now and the man God made for me, I am so grateful for God protecting me from myself. Settling in who I decided to become one with would have altered the course of my life completely, and it would have tainted the impact and effectiveness my life is supposed to have.

The same principle applies to business relationships. In 2016, I had the idea to start a podcast. I was looking to build a brand online, and, at the time, becoming a social media influencer was the way to do it. As I studied, I realized that the amount of time I would have to spend online and how much of my life I would have to share in order to be relevant didn't fit with the lifestyle I wanted to live. I wanted to build a brand but not at the expense of my day-to-day enjoyments and presence with those around me. Podcasting was, and still is, a very new platform. I was just getting started listening to podcasts and saw audio content as a future game-changer. As I studied my demographic, I also saw that my audience was learning about podcasting and actively looking for shows. This was the perfect opportunity for me.

Starting a podcast would mean that I would spend roughly three to five (or fewer) hours a week producing the content. Then, once it was done, I would be able to post it online, and it would be available immediately everywhere. What also stood out about podcasting is that there wasn't an algorithm that was determining who was able to find and access my content. It was as organic as creating content online was going to be. At the time, I had a youth organization that I had experienced success with, but I wanted to pivot my business. I decided to use my marketing acumen to build a coaching and consulting business that allowed me to help others build successful brands. I also saw podcasting as the perfect opportunity to take that online presence and turn my listeners into clients for my business.

With the concept in mind, I went on to develop the show.

This led me to reaching out to co-hosts and settling on a concept where we would talk about the journey of entrepreneurship and share the ups and downs in real time. The show launched in 2017, and it was an instant success. We were growing at a fast rate and accumulating thousands of listeners all over the world. As I was building this online presence, I was also building my relationship with God offline. I had decided to truly give my life to Him and be trusting and obedient, wherever that may lead me. I didn't realize that the faith I was building was going to translate into my entrepreneurial endeavors. As I grew my relationship with God, one of the first business instructions He gave me was to do my podcast alone. My co-host wasn't saved, and that wasn't a problem for me because I was barely saved myself. Even still, I didn't see a problem in having a business relationship and building a brand with someone who wasn't of the same belief system as me. I eventually ended up making the decision to break off our partnership and continue the podcast alone.

As I trusted God to guide my steps, I ended up with changing the name and premise of the show. Instead of discussing the journey of entrepreneurship, I would discuss the mindset of doing entrepreneurship under God's leadership—God as my CEO. The result? My listenership doubled within the first month. Since then, I have reached millions all over the world, completed a nationwide tour, and launched a media company—and the list goes on. My podcast is the reason you're reading this book today. I often wonder what would have happened if I would've left the show as it was. That partnership would've caused me to compromise my message and limited the impact that God wanted to make through me.

PRESSURE

Pressure to be open-minded leads to a concession of the principles of God. The manifestation of that concession can be allowing behaviors in your presence, home, church, or business that are contrary to the standard of righteousness. It shows itself as alliances, partnerships, and participations that could lead to immoral practices.

Revelation 2:13–15—The Message

"I see where you live, right under the shadow of Satan's throne. But you continue boldly in my Name; you never once denied my Name, even when the pressure was worst, when they martyred Antipas, my witness who stayed faithful to me on Satan's turf.

But why do you indulge that Balaam crowd? Don't you remember that Balaam was an enemy agent, seducing Balak and sabotaging Israel's holy pilgrimage by throwing unholy parties? And why do you put up with the Nicolaitans, who do the same thing?"

In the book of Revelation, John writes to the seven churches of Asia to commend them for their strengths and warn them about their flaws. In the preceding passage, he was speaking specifically to the church of Pergamum. Pergamum was a refined city that sat on the top of a hill and was the home of four idolatrous cults. The main god was called Asclepius. He was considered the god of healing. Many from all over traveled to seek healing from this god. As you can imagine, being a Christian in a city like this would bring great persecution and pressure to compromise to the idolatry. Artipus, who is mentioned in the verse that opens this section, was killed because of his unwillingness to give in to any pressure. Others in the church, though, tolerated the behavior and idolatry. Compromise was the rebuke of this church, and God was calling them to repent. This scripture makes me wonder how someone like Artipus can be loyal and faithful until his death, but others choose to settle. This shows the power of pressure. The city was surrounded by sin and idolatry. Many of us are surrounded by the same. The heaviness of pressure can be so excessive that you find yourself making concessions, but you have to stand firm. Stand firm in your beliefs and your way of living, no matter what.

I've seen pressure show up intensely when it comes to my business decisions. As I built my online presence via podcasting, I became an influencer. I was now seen as someone of importance because of the number of people who had subscribed to my show and teachings. This opened the door to many opportunities. Earlier, I talked about how I saw podcasting as a marketing vehicle to drive sales into the coaching business I was building. Well, when God instructed me to change the podcast, He also instructed me to shut down my business and to wait for what I was to do next. That wait turned into almost two years of feeling like an imposter in the online entrepreneur world because I had no business. Now that I am on the other side of it, I view this period as a training ground where God had to challenge me and test my loyalty. Was I going to be loyal to my ambition or loyal to pleasing Him?

The lack of consistent income during this time weighed heavily on me. I am a problem solver, and I knew that I could create a product, program, or something that would bring in consistent revenue. However, when I committed to doing things God's way, I had to stick to that decision. This pressure tempted me to compromise many times. I was presented with many opportunities that were in line with my revenue goals but not with God's instructions. These opportunities became so plentiful that I kept a spreadsheet of the amount of money I turned down on a weekly basis. The number got well into five figures, when I was making zero figures by doing things God's way. Even though I was feeling the financial strain of my obedience, I knew the deposits I was making in faith were going to birth more than what I turned down in due time. And even if they didn't, I was going to obey God anyway.

INCONSISTENCY

Solomon is considered to be the wisest man. When he became king and was given the choice of gifts from God, he chose to receive wisdom. This led him to have much success. Even in his wisdom, though, Solomon had a weak spot when it came to women. He married many women, either for political gain or his own lustful desires, and those unions ultimately led him to idolatry. It's human nature for us to have strengths and weaknesses. No one is perfect. And it's usually in those weak areas that we are tempted the most. Those temptations are what ultimately lead us to relax our standards. Solomon was wise and an accomplished leader. Unfortunately, that wisdom didn't translate to his weak areas, causing him to make foolish decisions. We are the same way. There may be areas where we are solid, strong, and uncompromising, but then there are other areas where we are lax and inconsistent. We must be knowledgeable of where our weaknesses are so that we can protect them and remain rational. Compromise creeps in when self-awareness isn't present. That lack of self-awareness then leads to an inconsistency in how we behave, and inconsistency leads to compromise.

In the following pages, I will demonstrate how being uncompromising and God being your stronghold work in tandem. As you continue reading, it'll become clear that the results you are seeking will ultimately come from Him.

CHAPTER 2

THE EXCELLENCE FALLACY

1 Peter 2:9–English Standard Version

But you are a chosen race, a royal priesthood, a holy nation, a people for his own possession, that you may proclaim the excellencies of him who called you out of darkness into his marvelous light.

2 Corinthians 4:7–King James Version

But we have this treasure in earthen vessels, that the excellency of the power may be of God, and not of us.

After you've divorced yourself from the human reasoning of settling, your actions must align with this new thought process and revelation. If you're reading this book, I believe you and I have a lot in common. I see you as someone who is an achiever. Someone who is high-performing, results driven, highly ambitious and focused on your goals. That's why you're here. You can buy into the idea of not settling, because you don't want to do that anyway. I would also bet good money on the notion that you've been called a perfectionist once or twice (or more) in your life. The pursuit of perfection is a trap that leaves many of us overwhelmed and unaccomplished. The core of being uncompromising is operating from supernatural strength and efficiency. But this pursuit of perfectionism ultimately holds us back because it perpetuates self-reliance and not total surrender to a God that is more brilliant than we could ever be. As a reformed perfectionist and overachiever, I realized that if my ambition and vigor were anchored in myself, I would spend the rest of my life collecting accolades and achievements and still never complete the very thing I was born to do.

Maybe you've accepted that perfection is an exhausting and unrealistic goal, so instead you've replaced perfectionism with excellence. I did the exact same thing. When I decided that I wanted to live a purpose-driven life and not just one full of trophies, I replaced my perfectionism with this idea of excellence. I even backed it up with scripture and justified my masked perfectionism with "working as if unto the Lord" (Colossians 3:23). This facade caught up with me after having my son and going back to work in my business. Prior to giving birth, I had planned to take a four-month maternity leave—a month before the baby arrived, to rest and prepare, then another three months to get acquainted with motherhood. After my maternity leave, I was so excited to get back to work in my business. Everyone told me not to rush back, but I love working so much that it feels like self-care. Once I got back, though, I realized just how hard my new life was going to be. I'm a problem solver by nature, and I believe that everything can be figured out. Though I knew that my new life would be an adjustment, I didn't think it would be that hard. I quickly received a reality check.

I got to a place in which I felt as if my day controlled me, and I didn't control my day. I had a baby who needed his mom, a husband who needed his wife, and a team who needed their leader. I felt as if I was drowning constantly and letting everyone down, including God. I beat myself up constantly because I felt as if I was letting God down by not being able to manage all of the things He'd blessed me with. I put this unrealistic expectation on myself to tough it out and not make excuses, because I had to be excellent. It all came to a head one day on my bedroom floor. I was working from home, and I pulled out my whiteboard to iron out some ideas I had for my business. Before I could even take the cap off of the marker, I broke down. I cried hysterically until my whiteboard was full of tears. I was so physically, mentally, and emotionally exhausted. I had given everything I had to be excellent, and though my business was thriving and my new baby was growing and developing well, I was depleted. I had nothing left for myself, and I knew that though I had the pieces to the life I always wanted, something was serious-ly wrong with how I was balancing it all and putting those pieces together.

BALANCE IS UNREALISTIC

According to Oxford Languages, balance is defined as an even distribution of weight enabling someone or something to remain upright and steady. Another definition says that balance is a condition in which different elements are equal or in the correct proportions. The key words in these definitions are even and equal. This insinuates that in order for us to achieve balance in our lives, our responsibilities must be even or equal. The reason many people aren't finding balance is because they're trying to make the weight of their many hats distribute evenly when they were never supposed to in the first place. For me, marriage, motherhood, and business do not all carry the same weight in my life. Does your career hold the same weight in your life as your family? I believe there is a hierarchy to the various areas of life and, because of this, balance will never be achieved. If you continue to try to reach this unattainable goal, you will never find true joy, happiness, or total life success. Let's throw the pursuit of balance out the window and say cheers to the stress that's going with it.

APPLY YOUR CHARACTERISTICS TO YOUR IDENTITY

The core of the scripture quoted at the top of the chapter is identity. The Bible tells us that we are made in the image of God and, because of that, the excellence that we exude through our work ethic is supposed to be an example on Earth of the greatness of Him and not the greatness of us. That's not to say that we should ignore the character traits we have as achieving people, but we are supposed to utilize our character as an opportunity to bring praise to the God that gave those traits to us. This was a pivotal shift in perspective for me as I was adjusting to my new normal. I was pouring from an empty cup, because I wasn't positioned in a way in which I was being replenished. I was positioned to where I was my own source. I didn't have enough to pour out in every area of my life, because I was being self-reliant and God-reliant.

In 2 Kings 4:1–7, we learn about the miracle of the oil vessels:

2 Kings 4:1–7—International Standard Version

Now there happened to be a certain woman who had been the wife of a member of the Guild of Prophets. She cried out to Elisha, "My husband who served you has died, and you know that your servant feared the Lord. But a creditor has come to take away my children into indentured servitude!" Elisha responded, "What shall I do for you? Tell me what you have in your house." She replied, "Your servant has nothing in the entire house except for a flask of oil." He told her, "Go out to all of your neighbors in the surrounding streets and borrow lots of pots from them. Don't get just a few empty vessels, either. Then go in and shut the door behind you, taking only your children, and pour oil into all of the pots. As each one is filled, set it aside." So she left Elisha, shut the door behind her and her children, and while they kept on bringing vessels to her, she kept on pouring oil. When the last of the vessels had been filled, she told her son, "Bring me another pot!" But he replied, "There isn't even one pot left." Then the oil stopped flowing. After this, she went and told the man of God what had happened. So he said, "Go sell the oil, pay your debt, and you and your children will be able to live on the proceeds."

This passage is not only an example of God providing in the form of resources for the woman to pay her debt. It's also an example of how God provided every time she positioned a vessel to be filled. It wasn't until the last vessel had been filled and she didn't bring any more that the oil stopped flowing. I believe that when we present ourselves as vessels to the Lord, He will fill us up and give us what we need to navigate our everyday lives. We only stop being replenished when we stop going to the source to be filled.

EXCELLENCE IS FRUIT

John 15:1–8—New International Version

"I am the true grapevine, and my Father is the gardener. He cuts off every branch of mine that doesn't produce fruit, and he prunes the branches that do bear fruit so they will produce even more. You have already been

pruned and purified by the message I have given you. Remain in me, and I will remain in you. For a branch cannot produce fruit if it is severed from the vine, and you cannot be fruitful unless you remain in me. Yes, I am the vine; you are the branches. Those who remain in me, and I in them, will produce much fruit. Apart from me, you can do nothing. Anyone who does not remain in me is thrown away like a useless branch and withers. Such branches are gathered into a pile to be burned. But if you remain in me and my words remain in you, you may ask for anything you want, and it will be granted! When you produce much fruit, you are my true disciples. This brings great glory to my Father."

When I looked up the biblical definition of excellence, I found that the Hebrew definition of the word is "fruit." I found this interesting because the Holy Spirit immediately reminded me of the preceding scripture. The foundation of achieving total life success is being properly positioned. It's the prioritization of your faith in God over your faith in yourself. It's the acknowledgment that you have above-average capabilities that have gotten you far in life, but the way that your life is going to operate in harmony is through surrendering control. Fruit is produced when we lock into the Father and operate from a place where we allow Him to flow through us, our endeavors, and our decisions. This fruit is true excellence, because it's evidence of God's divine capabilities and not our own. I've seen excellence show up as fruit in both my motherhood and business journeys.

MOTHERHOOD

I have always wanted to be a mom. As a child, I'd always seen myself as being very successful in business, as well as having a full family life. I wanted a big house with a pool in the backyard, a handsome husband who is successful in his own right, and multiple children who are happy, loved, and well taken care of. It never occurred to me that this dream may not be my reality until a hint came in college.

During my senior year, I was in a relationship and ended up getting pregnant unexpectedly. I was devastated because I was not ready to be a parent and did not know how I was going to provide for my unborn child. I eventually accepted my reality and began to get excited about my dream of motherhood coming true, even if it wasn't under ideal circumstances. When I went to my first OB-GYN appointment, we discovered that there was no embryo. The doctor proceeded to tell me that I was facing one of two scenarios. Either I was super-early along, or I was miscarrying. I held onto hope because I couldn't wrap my mind around having a miscarriage. A miscarriage, at the time, sounded like something was wrong with me, and I was not emotionally ready to consider that. Eventually, that pregnancy did end in a miscarriage.

It was very difficult for me, but I dealt with my emotions and moved on. I resolved in my heart that early miscarriages are very common and that it didn't mean my dream wouldn't happen. My world got turned upside down, though, when that was not the last time I heard a doctor tell me that my pregnancy wouldn't continue. After I got married, my husband and I didn't want to wait long to start our family. Once we got back from the honeymoon, we began trying, and I ended up getting pregnant pretty quickly. I was so excited to get those two lines on the pregnancy test that I immediately called my husband and all of my closest family members. Everyone was overjoyed with the news that we would be adding a new baby to the family. I made an appointment with my OB-GYN, and my appointment almost went identical to the last. We followed up with blood work a few times to confirm whether my pregnancy was progressing. After a couple of weeks, I got the call that I was having another miscarriage.

This miscarriage was even more heartbreaking, because I felt that I had finally done things right. I was married, I was living for God, and I was the most obedient I had ever been. But, unfortunately, that doesn't make us immune to tough times. I gave myself twenty-four hours to feel the feels and promised God and myself that I would pull it together and not lose faith, and that God would honor my dream of having my family. After that miscarriage, I began to put my faith into action. I started taking prenatal vitamins every day, I bought a pregnancy tea that was said to strengthen the uterus, I bought a onesie with 1 Samuel 1:27 on it and prayed that one day the child God blessed me with would wear it. Every morning, I anointed my belly, prayed over myself, decreed that my womb is blessed, and declared Psalm 113:9 over my body. I put my faith, my hope, and all of my trust in the God that I knew performed miracles. Since this was my second miscarriage, my OB-GYN asked me if I wanted to have some tests run to see why this may be happening. My emotions wanted to oblige, but my spirit instantly said, "No." I told the doctor that I would think about it and get back to her.

When I prayed about it, I asked God why was He telling me "No" when he blessed us with doctors to be able to run tests and solve problems such as these. He told me very clearly that He was going to provide this and that He didn't need help. He told me not to give into my emotions or temptations to have tests run and to just trust Him. I called my doctor back, thanked her for wanting to look into the matter and declined any further testing. A few months passed, and I was overjoyed to find out that I was pregnant again. My faith had worked! I did everything I knew to do spiritually to produce this blessing, and I was obedient in not having any tests done. In my mind, pregnancy number three was the one that would be viable, and I would have an amazing testimony to share.

The day of my first doctor's appointment for this pregnancy, I started spotting, and I immediately knew what was happening. That doctor's appointment went exactly like the others. I felt as if I was in a tormenting nightmare. My heart was barely healed from the last miscarriage, and it broke to pieces again as I learned this pregnancy, which I had so much hope for, would also end. I remember looking at my husband, who was feeling so defeated. The one thing that he desired over all, legacy, was the one thing I had not been able to give him.

My motherhood journey came down to two factors that I believe are the foundation or prerequisites of living uncompromisingly: decisions and perseverance.

My doctor asked again if I would like to get tests done, and I had to make a choice. Was I going to continue to choose God, or was I going to give in to what my reality said? I chose God and His way. I declined and decided that just because my reality wasn't adding up to what I was believing, I wasn't going to lose confidence in what I was hoping for and assurance about what hadn't been manifested yet (Hebrews 11:1). I wish I could tell you that choosing God was easy. It wasn't. This was the most vulnerable and risky "Yes" that I could have given Him. But I did it. I was relentless in that my story was going to be one that God got the glory for. Not me, not science, but Him. What came next, I believe, was another test to see if I was indeed settled in that choice. I got an email from a potential sponsor for my podcast. This sponsor was a family planning company that provided fertility testing kits. They wanted to sponsor my show. I would have to utilize the service and speak to my experience within the advertisement. Here I was again, being offered testing that I wanted—and it potentially could've told me why I was having recurrent miscarriages. Only this time, a check was attached to it.

I am still a businesswoman, so I negotiated. I told the sponsor that I would do the advertisement, but I would not be able to utilize the service and provide an endorsement. They agreed, and I was able to do the ad without compromising on my decision to leave my fertility to the Lord. A couple of months later, I got pregnant for the fourth time. This time, my doctor's appointment was polar opposite from the last three. My ultrasound showed that a healthy embryo with a strong heartbeat was growing completely normal inside me. My pregnancy lasted to term and, on May 16, 2020, I gave birth to a beautiful and healthy baby boy.

As I write this, I have no idea how I made it through all of that. But I am glad I did, because I can confidently say now that my son is the fruit of God's excellence. My future children are proof of His excellence. My perseverance is fruit that His grace is sufficient and that His strength is made perfect in my weakness (2 Corinthians 12:9–10). Science can't get the glory for this, the doctor can't get the glory for this, and I can't get the glory for this—because God did it. He stayed true to His promise to me, and because I was unyielding in my commitment to His way and got out of His way, I am able to proclaim His greatness with my story.

IN BUSINESS

At my company, Anchored Media, I develop and produce podcasts. I am also the host of my own show on the network. Since I have a faith-based company, I have to move not only using my business acumen, but I have to operate under the direction of the Holy Spirit. I call this concept "making God the CEO." Since I have chosen to do business this way, it sometimes feels as if I am starting at a disadvantage. When it comes to creating a successful podcast, we have proven frameworks and strategies that have allowed us to take shows from zero listens to hundreds of thousands of listeners. But when it comes to my podcast, some of those strategies have to get tabled in order for me to be obedient in the way that God wants my show to operate. For example, a common strategy to increase podcast listenership is having guests with active audiences on the show. It gives the guest the opportunity to spread their message and get in front of a new audience while allowing the podcaster to capitalize on their fans. Some shows even do what's called podcast swaps, in which podcasters are guests on each other's shows in order to increase each other's listenership.

With my podcast, *Blessed + Bossed Up*, I do not use this strategy. I have a rule that I do not interview people on my show whom I do not know personally. This allows me to maintain the integrity of my platform, and it honestly makes for a better interview most of the time. By making this decision, I am making my task of increasing listeners harder because I am not taking advantage of a proven method to reach my goal. The great thing about doing things God's way and looking for opportunities to proclaim His excellencies in business is that His way may not make sense to conventional knowledge, but it is always effective. My podcast has reached millions of people all over the world without having to compromise my integrity in any way because of industry best practices. As we continue to reach new territory, every new level is creating an opportunity to be a testimony of God's faithfulness and ability to make my name and business great. What seems on the surface as a setback is actually a setup for success.

Galatians 5:22–23—New International Version

But the fruit of the Spirit is love, joy, peace, forbearance, kindness, goodness, faithfulness, gentleness and self-control. Against such things there is no law.

Excellence is not about how well we can perform but rather how many opportunities we take advantage of to prove God's sovereignty and embody the fruit of the spirit.

CHAPTER 3

PREVENT PERFORMANCE AND UNLOCK OBEDIENCE

Isaiah 29:13-14—The Message

The Master said: "These people make a big show of saying the right thing, but their hearts aren't in it. Because they act like they're worshiping me but don't mean it, I'm going to step in and shock them awake, astonish them, stand them on their ears. The wise ones who had it all figured out will be exposed as fools. The smart people who thought they knew everything will turn out to know nothing."

1 Samuel 15:22-23—The Message

Then Samuel said,
Do you think all God wants are sacrifices—
  empty rituals just for show?
He wants you to listen to him!
Plain listening is the thing,
  not staging a lavish religious production.
Not doing what God tells you
  is far worse than fooling around in the occult.
Getting self-important around God
  is far worse than making deals with your dead ancestors.
Because you said No to God's command,
  he says No to your kingship.

The key to your success in God's way is obedience. When you're an achieving person, performance can sometimes make you feel like you're being obedient, but it's really just a front. Just like what we went over in the last chapter, that excellence is masked perfectionism, *performance is simulated obedience.* When I first got saved, I didn't truly give my life to God. I confessed with my mouth and believed in my heart that Jesus died on the cross for my sins, but I didn't see a transformation in how I lived on a daily basis because I didn't have the tools to actually live a righteous life. Instead, I felt I was met in church with a performance playbook. A rigid set of religious rules that made me look Christ-like based on my ability to adhere to them, but did nothing to assist me in living a life of purpose. The rules were clear, and the judgment, if those rules weren't followed, was harsh. The variation of the rule book differs between denominations, cultures, and communities, but the root of performance is present in them all. In my experience, I was taught how to act, but I was not given the tools to truly transform. This left me ill-equipped for my assignment in this world, and it was a nature I had to unlearn in order to be successful. I was taught how to obey a system, but I needed to learn how to obey my Savior.

PERFORMANCE VS. OBEDIENCE

Deuteronomy 28:1–12—New International Version

If you fully obey the Lord your God and carefully follow all his commands I give you today, the Lord your God will set you high above all the nations on earth. All these blessings will come on you and accompany you if you obey the Lord your God: You will be blessed in the city and blessed in the country. The fruit of your womb will be blessed, and the crops of your land and the young of your livestock—the calves of your herds and the lambs of your flocks. Your basket and your kneading trough will be blessed. You will be blessed when you come in and blessed when you go out. The Lord will grant that the enemies who rise up against you will be defeated before you. They will come at you from one direction but flee from you in seven. The Lord will send a blessing on your barns and on everything you put your hand to.

The Lord your God will bless you in the land he is giving you. The Lord will establish you as his holy people, as he promised you on oath, if you keep the commands of the Lord your God and walk in obedience to him. Then all the peoples on earth will see that you are called by the name of the Lord, and they will fear you. The Lord will grant you abundant prosperity—in the fruit of your womb, the young of your livestock, and the crops of your ground—in the land he swore to your ancestors to give you. The Lord will open the heavens, the storehouse of his bounty, to send rain on your land in season and to bless all the work of your hands. You will lend to many nations but will borrow from none. The Lord will make you the head, not the tail. If you pay attention to the commands of the Lord your God that I give you this day and carefully follow them, you will always be at the top, never at the bottom. Do not turn aside from any of the commands I give you today, to the right or to the left, following other gods and serving them.

In Deuteronomy, there are a series of speeches given by Moses to the new generation of Israelites getting ready to enter into the Promised Land. The generation before them who were saved from captivity in Egypt consistently disobeyed God and did not have faith. Their rebelliousness caused them to wander for forty years until their generation died off and God started over with the new generation. Moses was teaching this new generation the laws that were given at Mt. Sinai and informing them how to live in this Promised Land full of various forms of idolatry. When we get to the chapter above,

Moses is presenting them with an ultimatum and telling them the outcomes if they're obedient and the consequences of disobedience. Since we're talking about obedience here, I want you to see for yourself what happens when you obey God. We often hear these things preached in sermons, but the prerequisite to these blessings is often left out. These blessings are promised to you *if* you obey God. Earlier I said that performance is simulated obedience. It gives the look and feel that you're being used by God without the transformative power that only true devotion can provide. It feels good, but the work and decision-making that is supposed to accompany your faith isn't there. Without the work and decision-making, you ultimately end up in disobedience, and there are consequences for that (see Deuteronomy 28:15–68).

Deuteronomy 30:15–20—New International Version

See, I set before you today life and prosperity, death and destruction. For I command you today to love the Lord your God, to walk in obedience to him, and to keep his commands, decrees, and laws; then you will live and increase, and the Lord your God will bless you in the land you are entering to possess.

Though this may be the Old Testament, the core wisdom is still relevant: there are blessings and benefits attached to your obedience, devotion, and dedication to the Lord. Blessings that can only be unlocked through action and not performance.

THE ROADBLOCKS
TO OBEDIENCE

As high-performing women, we are driven by results. We want our efforts to produce our desired outcomes. This makes us easily susceptible to becoming performative, especially in our walk with God and pursuit of total life success through Him. Performing prohibits us from truly being excellent because, remember, excellence is fruit. The difference between fruit and the results we're used to getting is the manufacturer of it. Our nature to bring about accomplishments can easily send us back to declaring the excellencies of ourselves and not of Him. Before we can get to a place where we've mastered making room for God to manifest miracles or bear much fruit, we must create a strategy that keeps our human nature in check and out of His way. I don't want to just teach you how to achieve total life success, I want to teach you how to maintain it. If I only inspire you through these pages, I have failed. It's my goal that you have a set system for an abundant life that you can refer to and customize to your unique life. Let's break down three roadblocks to obedience and, more importantly, how we can overcome them.

James 1:22—New Living Translation

But don't just listen to God's Word. You must do what it says. Otherwise, you are only fooling yourselves.

PRIDE

Proverbs 16:18—The Message

First pride, then the crash—
the bigger the ego, the harder the fall.

The Oxford Languages definition of pride: a feeling of deep pleasure or satisfaction derived from one's own achievements, the achievements of those with whom one is closely associated, or from qualities or possessions that are widely admired. The reason why many get stuck in performance is because performance elicits feedback from the audience, and—if it's positive—it's an ego booster. It's an ego booster when you preach a sermon and get many "amens" from the congregation. Double points if you get a standing ovation and hand claps. It's gratifying to get likes, positive comments, and five-star reviews on your social media pages and website. It's human nature to want to be loved and received well by others. However, as people of faith, we have to maintain control over our human nature and make it subject to the rules of righteousness.

Pride doesn't always feel negative or like a roadblock to obedience, because it's a positive emotional response to something you have a connection to. For example, you may take pride in what you do for a living or pride in taking care of your family and household. These things make you happy and you have a positive connection to them. The reason why pride is a problem, even though it elicits positive emotions, is that the foundation is self. You take pride in what you do because

---

it makes you feel worthy and useful. Your accomplishments bring about validation and confidence. Your pride in your family and household brings praise and validation that feed your inward desire for approval. Pride is rooted in self, and for as long as your pleasure and contentment are anchored in you and not God, it will always get in the way of being obedient and receiving the blessings that come from that obedience.

So how do we maintain the happiness that pride brings without it being anchored in self? You replace it with joy. Joy is biblically defined as the awareness of God's grace. Oxford Languages defines it as a feeling of great pleasure and happiness. There is overlap between pride and joy, and I believe that's why they're often used together. The overlap is the emotions, but the difference is in the source of that emotion. Pride is happiness that is initiated by self. Joy is happiness that is initiated by the awareness of God's goodness. Pride comes before a fall, and joy comes before obedience.

BUSYNESS

Pride can often show itself in this next roadblock to obedience: busyness. As women who wear multiple hats, there's always something to do. However, when we plan our days so detailed in order to get everything done, we are scheduling based on our capacity instead of moving at the pace of grace. If you have it all figured out, planned out, and organized down to the smallest detail, where is the room for God to intervene? The benefit of having the Holy Spirit is that we have a guide and a teacher in real time, looking to direct our steps. But how can He do that if we're moving ahead of Him and have made our lives so noisy that we don't even see or hear His instruction? In order to be obedient, we have to hear the instructions. It's important that when you plan, you make room for God so that you don't get ahead of Him.

Let's take a look at Abraham and one of the most radical and prompt acts of obedience recorded.

Genesis 22—New Living Translation

Some time later, God tested Abraham's faith. "Abraham!" God called. "Yes," he replied. "Here I am. "Take your son, your only son—yes, Isaac, whom you love so much—and go to the land of Moriah. Go and sacrifice him as a burnt offering on one of the mountains, which I will show you." The next morning Abraham got up early. He saddled his donkey and took two of his servants with him, along with his son, Isaac. Then he chopped wood for a fire for a burnt offering and set out for the place God had told him about. On the third day of their journey, Abraham looked up and saw the place in the distance. "Stay here with the donkey," Abraham told the servants. "The boy and I will travel a little farther. We will worship there, and then we will come right back." So Abraham placed the wood for the burnt offering on Isaac's shoulders, while he himself carried the fire and the knife. As the two of them walked on together, Isaac turned to Abraham and said, "Father?" "Yes, my son?" Abraham replied. "We have the fire and the wood," the boy said, "but where is the sheep for the burnt offering?"

*"God will provide a sheep for the burnt offering, my son,"
Abraham answered. And they both walked on together.
When they arrived at the place where God had told him
to go, Abraham built an altar and arranged the wood on
it. Then he tied his son, Isaac, and laid him on the altar
on top of the wood. And Abraham picked up the knife to
kill his son as a sacrifice. At that moment, the angel of the
Lord called to him from Heaven, "Abraham! Abraham!"
"Yes," Abraham replied. "Here I am!" "Don't lay a hand
on the boy!" the angel said. "Do not hurt him in any way,
for now I know that you truly fear God. You have not
withheld from me even your son, your only son." Then
Abraham looked up and saw a ram caught by its horns in
a thicket. So he took the ram and sacrificed it as a burnt
offering in place of his son. Abraham named the place
Yahweh-Yireh (which means "the Lord will provide"). To
this day, people still use that name as a proverb: "On the
mountain of the Lord it will be provided."*

*Then the angel of the Lord called again to Abraham from
heaven. "This is what the Lord says: Because you have
obeyed me and have not withheld even your son, your
only son, I swear by my own name. I will certainly bless
you. I will multiply your descendants beyond number,
like the stars in the sky and the sand on the seashore.
Your descendants will conquer the cities of their enemies.
And through your descendants all the nations of the
earth will be blessed—all because you have obeyed me."*

Can we have an honest moment? I don't think if God told me to go and sacrifice my son that I would've handled it like Abraham. Even if I obeyed, there would have been a lot more text about my temper tantrum and back talk to God about His instruction. In this text, Abraham and his wife Sarah had believed God would give them a child for many years. They had been waiting for the promise for so long that Sarah agreed to let Abraham impregnate the servant because she doubted that God would come through for her in this area. But God kept His promise and Sarah gave birth to Isaac in her old age. We're unsure of exactly how old she was when she gave birth, but it was in her nineties. Abraham was 100 years old when Isaac was born.

Being instructed to sacrifice your child under any circumstances is devastating, but I can imagine the amount of confusion that Abraham had when given this instruction after waiting so long for the promise to be fulfilled. I give this brief backstory because I want you to put yourself in the emotional state of Abraham; our emotions and attachments play into why we do or do not obey God. I have highlighted a few elements of the scripture to emphasize how Abraham was hearing and responding to God in real time. Abraham wasn't in prayer, worship, or quiet time when God called out to him. It was a regular day and he was minding his business, when the Lord spoke and gave him specific instructions. The next morning, he got up to obey the Lord's instructions. Abraham was a wealthy livestock owner, had a family, and I'm sure had plenty of things on his agenda to do the next day. Even still, he wasn't too prideful about his obligations to pivot and adjust his plans when the Lord was giving him instructions: He wasn't too busy for God. Sometimes our schedule can prompt internal excuses when God is trying to lead us in a different direction.

It's important to take note of the fact that Abraham obeyed with no hesitation and no contingencies. He was willing to sacrifice his plans and a very important person to him (his son) to obey God. If that's not an inspiring example of radical obedience, I don't know what is. God didn't want Abraham to sacrifice his son, He wanted to build his character. He wanted to deepen his faith even more. It's important for us to realize on our own faith journeys that fire, when initiated by God, is a refinement process. It isn't meant to consume you but rather to cleanse, polish, and perfect. We see at the end of the story Abraham's reward for his obedience, but I believe what's more important is that he obeyed without even knowing what the reward would be. He obeyed simply because God said so, and he made himself available to hear and act when God spoke in real time.

A couple of years ago, before the baby, I wanted to plan a big trip to celebrate my husband's birthday. One of our favorite things to do together is travel and create new memories and experiences. I decided that it would be a perfect opportunity for us to travel to London, as I'd never been to Europe before. It was soccer season, and his favorite team would be playing in London during his birthday week, so it was perfect. I booked the flights, arranged for us to stay with his cousin, and even got tickets for all of us to attend the game. At this point, I felt like wife of the year. A few months after making the arrangements, we found out we were expecting our son. The trip seemed to be even more divinely aligned because it would be one of our last travel experiences before becoming parents. December came around, and it was a few weeks before we were set for departure. I had everything planned out: My Amazon cart was full of items to make me comfortable on a seven-hour flight while pregnant, and I was finalizing all the details to make this trip a success.

One morning as I was making a list for some last-minute items, I heard God say, "Don't go." I wish I could say that I immediately cancelled everything as I'd imagine Abraham would do, but I didn't. I tried to ignore what I was hearing and continued with planning. God, being the gentleman that He is, continued to tell me, "Don't go." After a few days, I decided that I had to listen to what God was saying and not go on the trip. I went from feeling like wife of the year to feeling embarrassed that I had to tell my husband we needed to cancel the trip we'd both been looking forward to. I told him that I didn't know why, but I believe God is telling me that we need to stay home. My husband was obviously disappointed, but he trusted me and he trusted God. That was December 2019, which is the timeframe where the earliest cases of the coronavirus are said to be recorded. I believe that God was protecting me, my husband, and our unborn child from a virus that caused a global pandemic that we are still experiencing as I write this book. This virus has taken the lives of millions of people all over the world. There is no way I could've planned for that. However, I serve a God that knows all things, and by obeying him, I am always operating in my best interest.

When you're planning your day and going about your everyday life, I encourage you to never be too busy for God and to always act on what you hear.

PEOPLE-PLEASING

Cambridge Dictionary defines a people pleaser as someone who cares a lot about whether other people like him or her and wants others to approve of his or her actions. Some individuals have personality types that prefer to avoid conflict and often end up people-pleasing at the expense of themselves. Even if this isn't your personality type, we live in a world in which we are groomed to care and put value into the opinions and approval of others. Pictures you post on social media leave room for likes and comments, which is a form of approval. Subscribers to online platforms are indicative of content, and the person creating the content wants to feel accepted by the audience. This acceptance is then translated into a monetary value as brands pay to be placed in front of consumers who place value in the recommendations of the influencer. It's difficult not to have a desire to please people in a society in which acceptance pays beyond just personal gratification. But as believers, we must keep to the forefront of our mind and align our decisions with the fact that it is our responsibility to please God and not people. Our loyalty can't be divided.

If you're someone who finds themselves people-pleasing, be it in the form of business decisions or in personal commitments, I want you to ask yourself, "Is this decision demonstrating my loyalty to God or my loyalty to the world or people?" You must choose.

It's important to note that loyalty to God also means loyalty to yourself. Love, joy, peace, and goodness are all fruits of the Spirit (Galatians 5:22–23). God has also given us a spirit of power and love and a sound mind (2 Timothy 1:7). I want to be clear that your loyalty and commitment to God aren't just an obligation but also access to freedom.

I believe that a couple of my personal strengths are that I am really good at setting boundaries and being decisive. My yes is yes and my no is no. I've been like this my whole life so my family and friends are used to it and respect it, even if they don't always agree with my boundaries and decisions. There have been times, though, when it's been hard to apply this aspect of my personality to business. When I first started podcasting, I would obsess over things such as reviews and analytics. I was constantly in tune with feedback in some way and making adjustments to please my audience. This worked for a while because I was able to carefully monitor my key performance indicators and adjust our marketing efforts, so that we could see the numbers and favorable feedback we were looking for. However, when I decided to do business God's way, I had to find a way to still be an efficient marketer while ensuring my loyalty to God wasn't being compromised. What that looked like was putting clear boundaries in place. The first boundary put in place, which I mentioned earlier, was not doing interviews.

The second was that the audience wouldn't dictate the main show content. When I speak on my podcast, I look at it as an assignment and an opportunity to say what God instructs me to say for the forty-five minutes or so that I am on the microphone. It may or may not be relevant to world events or pop culture, but it will always be in tune with the Holy Spirit. To still appease our audience, we've found other ways to create more content or be creative, such as utilizing

Instagram, YouTube, email, and bonus episodes. The result: My platform grew exponentially across these channels. This has translated into an increase not only in podcast listenership but an increase in people hearing the Word of God who would otherwise not have. In this instance, I was able to find a way to market effectively while still being obedient to God with my platform. It's easy to fall into the trap of doing things for others, but the way to overcome this roadblock and remain in obedience is to consistently check ourselves, our intentions, and our decisions.

Obeying God doesn't come naturally. It comes by actively listening for instructions and making a conscious decision to obey those instructions despite how you feel about it or what you have to give up to do it.

CHAPTER 4

PASSIONATE PATIENCE

Revelation 3:10—The Message

Because you kept my Word in passionate patience, I'll keep you safe in the time of testing that will be here soon, and all over the earth, every man, woman, and child put to the test.

The book of Revelation is a graphic depiction of the patterns of history and God's promise. It's a book of hope and warning. In the beginning of the book, John wrote letters to the seven churches of Asia that were experiencing persecution. In each letter, there was a commendation, a rebuke, and a call for action. In the preceding scripture, God, through John, was addressing the church of Philadelphia specifically. This was the only church that God did not have a rebuke for, and the action that he gave was to simply *hold on*. The other churches were being condemned for things like not being consistent in love, tolerating compromise, tolerating immorality, superficiality, and being lukewarm. God gave them all actions to repent and turn from their errors. I wonder how frustrating it must have been for the church of Philadelphia to be the one doing everything right, even amid intense persecution and having no instructions or strategy from God other than to hold on. The rebellious churches got a to-do list: repent, remember, don't fear, be diligent, and be faithful. But the church that never wavered was instructed to sit tight.

It's important that we address in this chapter something that many of us achieving women don't have a lot of: patience. We have to tackle this head on, because our inability to slow down could make or break not only our total life success, but our fulfillment of our purpose here on Earth and God's promise for our lives.

Highlight this: Patience propels us into the promise.

Patience is defined as the power or capacity to endure without complaint something difficult or disagreeable. It's one of the fruits of the spirit, and it's a core quality that we must exude to be in alignment with God. Patience keeps you at God's pace. Our purpose isn't meant to be microwaved, but we often allow the pressure we put on ourselves to push us off track. This pressure then produces a lot of busy work and the illusion that we're now gaining traction, but really, we're just running in place. Patience is an energy saver because it allows us to focus our efforts on what's productive and not just on staying busy—that's key for women who wear many hats. We don't want to be on a hamster wheel, we want to remain in His will, and that requires patience. I would like to offer a perspective that patience isn't something that always looks like stagnation, but rather patience can present itself as opportunity. I believe that patience provides three key freedoms: character-building, unlocked answers, and ammunition against opposition.

CHARACTER-BUILDING

Genesis 32:22–26—New Living Translation

During the night, Jacob got up and took his two wives, his two servant wives, and his eleven sons and crossed the Jabbok River with them. After taking them to the other side, he sent over all his possessions. This left Jacob all alone in the camp, and a man came and wrestled with him until the dawn began to break. When the man saw that he would not win the match, he touched Jacob's hip and wrenched it out of its socket. Then the man said, "Let me go, for the dawn is breaking!" But Jacob said, "I will not let you go unless you bless me."

The preceding text is an example of the grace of God. Grace is defined as God's unmerited favor. Jacob didn't deserve God's grace, but it was given to him anyway because of his determination. In the moment when he wrestled with God, he was in a very humbled state. Earlier on, he had deceived his father and robbed his brother of his inheritance. After getting a taste of his own medicine by being deceived by his uncle, a humbled Jacob returned to his homeland and wrestled with God. Jacob, after wrestling all night and getting injured in the process, still refused to give up until God blessed him. This persistence led God to bless Jacob and then change his name to Israel, which means "wrestles with God" or "God fights."

When we contend for the blessing through exercising patience and persistence, we are given a new identity in Christ. Jacob went from being conniving to steadfast in his pursuit of God's promise. He went from being selfish to a servant. Jacob's life is one worth studying because I believe that even though we may not consider ourselves to be deceitful, we have a lot more in common with Jacob, pre–wrestling match, than we think.

How often have you taken your desires into your own hands and done whatever it took to see them through? You may not have robbed your sibling of their inheritance, but have you ever robbed God of the opportunity to have authority over your life? Have you made decisions without praying? Have you relied on your intellect and skills and not on the Holy Spirit? I know I have. I am usually in an in-between stage of my life or goals when my self-reliance shows up and attempts to push me off of the path God has me on.

I decided to sign up for a mastermind program to grow

my personal brand and further establish myself as a credible, well-paid speaker. I already had a platform and was getting paid in the thousands to speak, but I wanted to get to the point where I was making over six-figures in just speaking alone. I did what I always do when I want to grow: I invested in myself. I learned a lot of valuable information in the program, but I started to realize that a good eighty-five percent of it was actively applying. There came a point in the program where it became less about how I can take this knowledge and apply it to how God wants me to show up as a professional speaker and more about how well I can fit into the box that was being taught to me. I became frustrated with this realization because I had high expectations. I was enthusiastic about being able to learn frameworks that would take me from where I was to where I wanted to be, but the deeper I got into it, I realized there was a conflict between the organization's systems and God's assignment for me. As I took my frustrations to prayer, I realized that I already had what I needed prior to the program. I just needed to sit tight. By leaning into my ambition more than the Holy Spirit, I almost robbed God of the opportunity to get the glory for my success because I felt He wasn't moving fast enough. He put up a mirror to my unbelief that I didn't even know I had. That situation developed my character because it revealed a flaw within myself that, if not tamed, could cause me to unknowingly get off track.

UNLOCKED ANSWERS

Matthew 7:7–8—The Passion Translation

"Ask, and the gift is yours. Seek, and you'll discover. Knock, and the door will be opened for you. For every persistent one will get what he asks for. Every persistent seeker will discover what he longs for. And everyone who knocks persistently will one day find an open door.

I love the simplicity and straightforwardness of the teachings of Jesus. The preceding text is a very clear cause-and-effect that we can put our hope in when we pursue God. He honors our focus, commitment, and persistent pursuit of Him. When we exercise patience by continuing to seek Him, we find answers. If you haven't found the answers you need from God yet, keep knocking.

AMMUNITION AGAINST OPPOSITION

Nehemiah 6:15–16—New Living Translation

So on October 2, the wall was finished—just fifty-two days after we had begun. When our enemies and the surrounding nations heard about it, they were frightened and humiliated. They realized this work had been done with the help of our God.

Nehemiah was an incredible leader and a man of action. He learned that the wall in Jerusalem was in ruins, and it grieved him. So much so that he asked permission from his boss, King Artaxerxes, to go to Jerusalem to rebuild it. It was an "impossible" task, but he was determined to not just talk about how he felt but to do something to solve the problem that weighed so heavily on him. In building the wall, he received threats and was taunted and ridiculed. At every point of opposition, he responded in two ways: prayer and action. His steadfastness in the midst of adversity led to the job being completed in record time and his enemies having to eat their words and admit that God was with him.

Opposition of any kind is never a time to fold, rather a time to prove your faith with your perseverance. The vision always seems absurd until it's accomplished. Nehemiah had a vision, and he followed through. These are characteristics that we must embody in order to exercise passionate patience while we wait for God's promises to be fulfilled.

I remember the day I got the vision for Anchored Media so vividly. A friend of mine and I were accountability partners, helping each other to go deeper in our faith. We wanted to grow even closer to God and were helping each other get there. One day during our check-ins, we got to talking about business, and she shared with me some major goals she had and how she felt she was hitting a glass ceiling. I told her that some things only come through prayer and fasting (Matthew 17:21), so maybe we should go on a fast together so that she could get her breakthrough. She agreed, and we decided to fast that upcoming Monday. At the time I had things I was frustrated about as well, but I had the mindset that this fast wasn't about me—it was about my friend. I was determined to partner my faith with hers and intercede on her behalf.

Throughout the day, God gave me many encouraging words for her and some instructions to help her break that glass ceiling she was experiencing. At the end of the fast, I went into prayer one last time to thank God for the revelations He had given throughout the day. I had no idea that He was going to download an "impossible" vision for me. He gave me the whole blueprint for Anchored Media. The mission, the service offerings—everything. I had about ten pages of notes when it was all said and done. He also told me to do an event that we call the Find Your Voice Academy (FYVA), which is a multiday retreat and a group program to help new and aspiring podcasters build profitable platforms. After laying it all out, He told me to "go," and I immediately got to work. I had no idea what I was doing, and the opposition presented itself both internally and externally. I felt unqualified to build platforms for others, and I felt like I didn't have what it took to build a company to the magnitude in both reach and profitability that was on the pages of my prayer journal. I couldn't go to others for advice, because I didn't know anyone else building anything similar. Everyone thought I was crazy, because the vision didn't make sense. But I remembered Nehemiah and how he handled his struggles with prayer and action. So I did the same.

A few weeks later I introduced the FYVA retreat to the public, and it sold out in days. It sold out so quickly that we set another date for the next month, and that one sold out in a week. The event still continues to sell out in record time every time we do it. What's even better is that we've transformed small shows to ones charting on Apple Podcasts in countries all over the world. We've helped everyday people build massive platforms that not only make an impact but provide financial freedom. That experience made me realize that opposition will present itself whenever I'm walking by faith, but action, prayer, and perseverance are the keys to winning every time.

THE ADVERSARY TO PATIENCE

There is an innate characteristic that we possess as people that is constantly at conflict with our ability to be patient: instant gratification. Instant gratification is our desire to experience pleasure or fulfillment quickly. Our need to be satisfied without delay is a direct contradiction to our call to be passionately patient. We must recognize it so that we can actively tame this part of ourselves in order to stay within the will of God. Our flesh is always at war with our spirit. We are living in bodies that want to sin and fulfill its own needs. But as followers of Christ, we must exercise self-control and put the efficient measures in place to keep our flesh in alignment with our spirit. With instant gratification, the advancement of technology has only fueled this aspect of ourselves. If you want a ride, you can place an order on an app and someone will pick you up in minutes. If you want groceries, you can order them on an app and someone will shop for you and drop them off within two hours. If you want to know something or have a question answered, you can google it and find what you're looking for in seconds. This makes being patient even harder. But even though patience and perseverance may not be natural, they're possible.

The key to overcoming instant gratification and being patient boils down to your decisions. My mother used to say, "Life is choice-driven: We live and die by the choices we make." Success or failure isn't the result of some immense event but rather the result of the mundane decisions made on a daily basis. The same can be said with compromise. Getting to a space where you're settling for less than God's best isn't something that happens all of a sudden but rather one compromising decision at a time.

James 2:21–23—New Living Translation

Don't you remember that our ancestor Abraham was shown to be right with God by his actions when he offered his son Isaac on the altar? You see, his faith and his actions worked together. His actions made his faith complete. And so it happened just as the Scriptures say: "Abraham believed in God, and God counted him as righteous because of his faith." He was even called the friend of God.

Whenever instant gratification creeps in and you're pressed to remain patient, remember that it's your actions that make your faith complete. Consider every decision an opportunity to prove your faith.

THE PROMISES OF PATIENCE

It's important to understand that our patience will never be in vain. God has promises stored up for those who obey Him and are committed to both His plan and His pace. As you learn to slow down and get on pace with God, be assured that your patience will unlock these three key promises: eternal life, victory against the enemy, and blessings on Earth.

PROMISE #1: ETERNAL LIFE

1 Corinthians 9:24–27—The Message

You've all been to the stadium and seen the athletes race. Everyone runs; one wins. Run to win. All good athletes train hard. They do it for a gold medal that tarnishes and fades. You're after one that's gold eternally. I don't know about you, but I'm running hard for the finish line. I'm giving it everything I've got. No lazy living for me! I'm staying alert and in top condition. I'm not going to get caught napping, telling everyone else all about it and then missing out myself.

Galatians 6:7–10—New Living Translation

Don't be misled—you cannot mock the justice of God. You will always harvest what you plant. Those who live only to satisfy their own sinful nature will harvest decay and death from that sinful nature. But those who live to please the Spirit will harvest everlasting life from the Spirit. So let's not get tired of doing what is good. At just the right time, we will reap a harvest of blessing if we don't give up. Therefore, whenever we have the opportunity, we should do good to everyone—especially to those in the family of faith.

When you're patient and persevere, you win a gold medal of eternal life. Our obedience will produce blessings on Earth, but the biggest blessing of all is where we get to spend eternity. None of the things we accumulate on Earth can go with us to Heaven. Though it may feel restrictive to willingly endure, the reward is infinite.

PROMISE #2: VICTORY AGAINST THE ENEMY

Ephesians 6:10–20—King James Version

Finally, my brethren, be strong in the Lord and in the power of his might. Put on the whole armour of God, that ye may be able to stand against the wiles of the devil. For we wrestle not against flesh and blood but against principalities, against powers, against the rulers of the darkness of this world, against spiritual wickedness in high places. Wherefore take unto you the whole armour of God, that ye may be able to withstand in the evil day, and having done all, to stand. Stand therefore, having your loins girt about with truth, and having on the breastplate of righteousness; And your feet shod with the preparation of the gospel of peace; Above all, taking the shield of faith, wherewith ye shall be able to quench all the fiery darts of the wicked. And take the helmet of salvation, and the sword of the Spirit, which is the Word of God: Praying always with all prayer and supplication in the Spirit, and watching thereunto with all perseverance and supplication for all saints.

Usually when we see the preceding scripture, we emphasize the elements of the armor of God: the belt of truth, shoes of peace, helmet of salvation, shield of faith, breastplate of righteousness, and sword of the spirit. But an element that I believe is undervalued can be found in verse 13 when the writer instructs us to withstand, and when we have done all, to stand. When you withstand, you endure and persevere. In this passage, our persistence is just as important as putting on the armor. They go hand in hand. The only way we lose to the enemy's devices is if we cease to persist. Friend, never forfeit a fight that's fixed in your favor. Your patience unlocks the promise of victory.

PROMISE #3: BLESSINGS ON EARTH

Genesis 32:22–32—New Living Translation

During the night, Jacob got up and took his two wives, his two servant wives, and his eleven sons and crossed the

Jabbok River with them. After taking them to the other side, he sent over all his possessions. This left Jacob all alone in the camp, and a man came and wrestled with him until the dawn began to break. When the man saw that he would not win the match, he touched Jacob's hip and wrenched it out of its socket. Then the man said, "Let me go, for the dawn is breaking!" But Jacob said, "I will not let you go unless you bless me." "What is your name?" the man asked. He replied, "Jacob." "Your name will no longer be Jacob," the man told him. "From now on you will be called Israel, because you have fought with God and with men and have won." "Please tell me your name," Jacob said. "Why do you want to know my name?" the man replied. Then he blessed Jacob there. Jacob named the place Peniel (which means "face of God"), for he said, "I have seen God face-to-face, yet my life has been spared." The sun was rising as Jacob left Peniel, and he was limping because of the injury to his hip. Even today, the people of Israel don't eat the tendon near the hip socket because of what happened that night when the man strained the tendon of Jacob's hip.

Does this scripture look familiar? Earlier in the chapter, we discussed verses 22–26, in which Jacob was persistent in wrestling with God until He blessed him. I want you to pay attention to the result of that determination that came after the blessing. Simple, right? This life is not as complicated as we make it seem. When we are passionately patient, God blesses us.

In chapter two, I told you about my multiple miscarriages. I like to look at that season as my own wrestling with God moment. After every loss, I pleaded with God. I cried out to Him, and I mean ugly, snotty nose, puffy face cries. I turned down every test and everything offered to me to pinpoint the problem because I refused to accept anything but a blessing straight from God, the way that He said He would give it to me. I fought for months, and my healthy child is the result of that patience and perseverance.

HE IS PATIENT WITH US

John 3:1–21—New Living Translation

There was a man named Nicodemus, a Jewish religious leader who was a Pharisee. After dark one evening, he came to speak with Jesus. "Rabbi," he said, "we all know that God has sent you to teach us. Your miraculous signs are evidence that God is with you."

Jesus replied, "I tell you the truth, unless you are born again, you cannot see the Kingdom of God." "What do you mean?" exclaimed Nicodemus. "How can an old man go back into his mother's womb and be born again?" Jesus replied, "I assure you, no one can enter the Kingdom of God without being born of water and the Spirit. Humans can reproduce only human life, but the Holy Spirit gives birth to spiritual life.

So don't be surprised when I say, "You must be born again." The wind blows wherever it wants. Just as you can hear the wind but can't tell where it comes from or where it is going, so you can't explain how people are born of the Spirit." "How are these things possible?" Nicodemus asked. Jesus replied, "You are a respected Jewish teacher, and yet you don't understand these things? I assure you, we tell you what we know and have seen, and yet you won't believe our testimony. But if you don't believe me when I tell you about earthly things, how can you possibly believe me if I tell you about heavenly things? No one has ever gone to Heaven and returned. But the Son of Man has come down from Heaven. And as Moses lifted up the bronze snake on a pole in the wilderness, so the Son of Man must be lifted up, so that everyone who believes in him will have eternal life.

For this is how God loved the world: He gave his one and only Son, so that everyone who believes in him will not perish but have eternal life. God sent his Son into the world not to judge the world but to save the world through him. There is no judgment against anyone who believes in him. But anyone who does not believe in him has already been judged for not believing in God's one and only Son. And the judgment is based on this fact: God's light came into the world, but people loved the darkness more than the light, for their actions were evil. All who do evil hate the light and refuse to go near it, for fear their sins will be exposed. But those who do what is right come to the light so others can see that they are doing what God wants.

Jesus's meeting with Nicodemus shows that He doesn't just want us to be patient, but He's patient with us as well. Nicodemus had seen Jesus in action, and he had questions. Since He was a Pharisee, there was risk involved with this visit. Nicodemus showed humility when he decided to see Jesus despite the risk and ask questions. Jesus didn't condemn him for having questions but rather answered them so that Nicodemus could have understanding past what he was used to. Jesus was patiently trying to take him from his depth of knowledge of religion and enlighten him on relationships.

How many times have you given up because you had questions for God? With humility and a heart to understand, take those questions to God. He cares. He knows us, and He's patient with us too.

MORE SCRIPTURES TO HELP WITH PATIENCE

Romans 15:5—The Passion Translation

Now may God, the source of great endurance and comfort, grace you with unity among yourselves, which flows from your relationship with Jesus, the Anointed One.

Galatians 5:22–23—The Passion Translation

But the fruit produced by the Holy Spirit within you is divine love in all its varied expressions: joy that overflows, peace that subdues, patience that endures, kindness in action, a life full of virtue, faith that prevails, gentleness of heart, and strength of spirit. Never set the law above these qualities, for they are meant to be limitless.

Colossians 1:11—New Living Translation

We also pray that you will be strengthened with all his glorious power so you will have all the endurance and patience you need. May you be filled with joy.

Colossians 3:12—New Living Translation

Since God chose you to be the holy people he loves, you must clothe yourselves with tenderhearted mercy, kindness, humility, gentleness, and patience.

2 Timothy 3:10—New Living Translation

But you, Timothy, certainly know what I teach, and how I live, and what my purpose in life is. You know my faith, my patience, my love, and my endurance.

Titus 2:2—New Living Translation

Teach the older men to exercise self-control, to be worthy of respect, and to live wisely. They must have sound faith and be filled with love and patience.

James 5:10—New Living Translation

For examples of patience in suffering, dear brothers and sisters, look at the prophets who spoke in the name of the Lord.

2 Peter 3:15—New Living Translation

And remember, our Lord's patience gives people time to be saved. This is what our beloved brother Paul also wrote to you with the wisdom God gave him.

Friend, remember: Patience propels us into the promise.

It can be and will be difficult to persevere through whatever trials come your way, but you have to do it. It's the key to unlocking the blessings you want to see on Earth and the blessing of eternal life. Passionate patience brings peace to the process of our purpose. Continue to do your life God's way. Don't worry about anything; instead, pray about everything. Tell God what you need, and thank Him for all He has done. Then you will experience God's peace, which exceeds anything we can understand. His peace will guard your hearts and minds as you live in Christ Jesus (Philippians 4:6–7 NLT).

CHAPTER 5

YOUR VISION IS AT STAKE

Recently, my mother had to undergo emergency eye surgery in order to fix a retinal detachment. I started researching the matter to be the best support person possible for her in recovery. I went down a rabbit hole of research that led me to a revelation that a retinal detachment is also a metaphor for what happens in the spiritual realm that keeps many women of faith living a limited life. Your eye consists of many elements that work together to enable you to see. Your retina's job is to receive and organize visual information that, when communicated with your brain, facilitates your vision. A detachment happens when the retina is pulled away from its necessary position. This causes symptoms such as floaters, a dark shadow in your field of vision, or flashing light in one or both of your eyes. When your retina becomes detached, it's considered an emergency and must be fixed immediately, or you risk losing your vision altogether.

Serious stuff, right?

Now imagine how serious this is for the vision and foresight God has for your life. You are the retina in Heaven's agenda for you. You receive and organize visual information that, when communicated with God, facilitates your vision. A detachment happens when you are pulled away from your necessary position. This causes symptoms such as fear, anxiety, and compromise. When you are detached from God, it is considered an emergency, and it must be fixed immediately, or you put the assignment at risk altogether.

One of the most common causes of a retinal detachment is eye injury. This drove the metaphor home for me because it personified the severity of what happens when we are spiritually attacked.

Ephesians 6:12—New Living Translation

For we are not fighting against flesh-and-blood enemies, but against evil rulers and authorities of the unseen world, against mighty powers in this dark world, and against evil spirits in the heavenly places.

If the enemy can effectively get you out of your position and detach you from God, they can kill every dream you've worked hard for, the assignment, and plans God has for your life. When you give your life to Christ, you enter a battle against the enemy and their army who want to do everything in their power to turn you away from God and ultimately destroy you. It's a messy, below the belt, literal fight for your life. I'm not telling you this to scare you, but I would be remiss if I didn't warn you. Living this uncompromising life will come with opposition and a targeted attack on the vision God gave you. The enemy's job is to kill, steal, and destroy, but God has come so that we can have life and have it to the fullest (John 10:10). Understand that the enemy and God are by no means equal, but we must be mindful of the fight at hand so that we continue to proclaim our victory and maintain our sight. The higher you go with your purpose and the things of God, the more intense the opposition will be. Spoiler alert: You are built for this, and the victory is already won. You can and will have total life success in God's way, uncompromisingly.

In this chapter, we're going to focus specifically on this attack against your vision, because the longer these attacks go unresolved, the greater the risk of losing all you've been working so hard for—just as a detached retina, if unresolved, can cause a person to lose their vision altogether. To implement the efficiency system that I am going to lay out for you in chapter seven, you must have an unobstructed view. What's going to allow you to live a life of harmony is having a clear vision, given by God, that you're using as a blueprint for how you plan and navigate your everyday life. Let's explore a few of the tactics the enemy uses to inflict injury and cause us to detach from God.

EMOTIONS

1 Peter 5:8—New International Version

Be alert and of sober mind. Your enemy the devil prowls around like a roaring lion looking for someone to devour.

When you think of being sober, you may automatically think about being free from the influence of drugs and alcohol. But those aren't the only substances that intoxicate us. I would argue that emotions are just as dangerous, if managed improperly. When doing purpose work, we are emotionally invested. That's what makes us so passionate about what we do. When it comes to our family, we are emotionally invested—that's why we're so protective. I'm not asking you to be heartless. But I am challenging you to be intentional about being emotionally healthy overall, as well as about managing your emotions effectively day-to-day so that they don't become so blinding that they set you off course.

FEAR

2 Timothy 1:7—New Living Translation

For God has not given us a spirit of fear and timidity but of power, love, and self-discipline.

I believe that fear is an indicator of our humanity, but you can't allow it to distort your vision or paralyze you in any way. Fear is not of God because God is love, and perfect love casts out fear (1 John 4:18). The scripture goes on to say that the one who fears has not been perfected in love. I don't believe that as individuals we will ever be perfect, but we serve a perfect God. As we abide in Him and He abides in us, we are perfected in love; thus fully equipped, through Him do we eject fear completely. This is done through action, perseverance, and a decision to fully submit to and rely on God and His path.

ANXIETY

Philippians 4:6–7—New Living Translation

Don't worry about anything; instead, pray about every-thing. Tell God what you need, and thank him for all he has done. Then you will experience God's peace, which exceeds anything we can understand. His peace will guard your hearts and minds as you live in Christ Jesus.

Fear and anxiety forbid freedom.

Anxiety is an exacerbator of fear because it attaches false sce-narios and events to the already unpleasant emotion, making things worse. When fear is coupled with anxiety, it causes a paralyzing effect and makes a person who is meant to be bold, stagnant. Fear, anxiety, worry, and any other negative emotion put us in a prison of carnality and prevent us from giving ourselves permission to soar. This is why they're so effective in the enemy's arsenal. If they can make you too afraid, too nervous, and too emotionally intoxicated to persevere, they've won—and the souls attached to you remain lost.

Fear and anxiety would've kept me from becoming a mother if I gave into those emotions. Everything about my story pointed to me not being able to carry children, but I knew that it was God's will for me to do so. I remember when I got pregnant with my son, I got excited when I saw the positive pregnancy test, but I didn't allow myself to get too excited because of fear that my pregnancy would turn out like the others. I made my first doctor's appointment far out because I didn't want to deal with the heartbreak of another empty ultrasound photo and hearing that I was miscarrying once again. My fear and anxiety wanted me to experience ten months of stress and worry that something would go wrong. But I decided that I was going to apply the same faith I did before and trust that God would carry me as I carried my son to term.

The emotions of fear and anxiety work as a one-two punch, knocking you completely off path if you let them. Fear and anxiety can turn purpose into a prison if you let them. Don't.

NEGATIVE THOUGHTS

2 Corinthians 10:5—New International Version

We demolish arguments and every pretension that sets itself up against the knowledge of God, and we take captive every thought to make it obedient to Christ.

A negative mind will never produce positive results, and a limited mindset is still negative. Your input dictates your output. Remember how we talked about strongholds in chapter one? A stronghold first presents itself in your mind, and it becomes rooted the moment you agree with it. When a pessimistic thought first comes into your mind, the second you agree with it and don't immediately throw it out, it becomes true *to you.* A lie can be true to you if you believe it. That's why this tactic of the enemy against your vision is so effective. If you believe that you have to sacrifice yourself for your children, that will be your truth. If you believe that you can't have a successful career and family at the same time, that will be your truth. But if you dared to believe the opposite— that harmony in your career, your home, and within yourself is realistic—it will become achievable. Before we can even get into the system of how to do that, you must believe it and divorce yourself from the limiting thoughts and beliefs that have held you back up until this point.

One of my most listened-to podcast episodes ever is called, "Who told you that?" In that episode, I spoke about the importance of getting to the root of our mental influences so that we can rewire our thought life to align with God's Word and His plans for us. Before there is a thought, there is an influence. Any negative thinking we experience is usually the result of a negative influence being let in somewhere. As you go about living an uncompromising life, you must evaluate what led you to compromise in the first place. What is the source of your doubt and unbelief? Then, ask yourself, "What in my life is currently still feeding this doubt and unbelief?" Once you understand that, you can do the work to correct.

WHAT IF VS. WHAT IF I DON'T

I don't think anyone needs too much convincing about why negative thinking is a problem, so I want to offer you an exercise to serve as a solution to counteract the negativity your mind may want to take. "What if" is a destructive rabbit hole that we can find ourselves in that is full of self-doubt and worry and serves no good purpose in achieving success. But these "what if" thoughts and statements are how negative thoughts often come. I want you to change that by adding two simple words to the end: "What if I don't?" If you don't do the thing God has called you to do, what does that mean for the impact your life is supposed to have? What does that mean for the generational blessings your grandchildren and great-grandchildren are supposed to experience? What does that mean for the lives attached to your obedience that will only find God through you? So instead of jumping off the deep end of worry via "what ifs," venture into the land of positivity and possibilities and asking, "What if I don't?"

PEOPLE

1 Corinthians 15:33—New International Version

Do not be misled: "Bad company corrupts good character."

An important part of maintaining a positive thought life is to put safeguards in place around what you allow yourself to take in. If you're constantly surrounded by people who have settled in any way, settling becomes normal. If the relationships in your life are full of people who have limited mindsets instead of growth mindsets, they will put their limitations on you. One of my favorite quotes comes from the rapper Jay-Z. He stated in an interview, "Don't listen to anyone, everyone is scared." This is a quote that I remember often when I am making big decisions that I feel like no one understands. It also helps when I confide in people and they don't seem to understand where I am coming from.

I went to a birthday dinner this year and in typical "new mom" questioning, I got asked about when I was going to have another baby. I made a comment that I wouldn't even consider having more kids until I hired a nanny. My answer was met with multiple variations of "I have three kids, I work full-time, and I don't have a nanny." It was as if my desire to hire help took away from my competencies as a wife and a mother. If I'm being honest, I initially took these comments to heart. I started to internalize that maybe I do need to do it all in order to have it all, but that was a lie. It was a limitation being put on me by people who I'm sure would hire help if they had the resources.

This superwoman complex is one that keeps many women overworked and unfulfilled for the majority of their lives. I did not want to fall into that trap. I walked into that dinner confident and left questioning myself, all by allowing the limited mindset of others impact my own thinking. I ended up calling a good friend of mine to vent. I was telling her how overwhelmed I was and that we were considering hiring a nanny to have some in-home care for our son during the day to free me up to work on my business, but I was thinking about not moving forward with it after the dinner conversation.

My friend quickly reminded me to never apologize for creating a structure for my family that allows us to operate at our best. She affirmed me and reminded me that my life is my own. My family is my own, and though it may be great to have people cheer you on and understand your every decision, it's not realistic. But it is up to me to build a life that I love, and it will be me at the end of my life giving an account for how I managed all God blessed me with. I will say this same advice to you as it relates to your negative thoughts or dealing with limited thinking: Your mindset, your thought life, and your mental health is yours to maintain and protect. Fix your thoughts on what is true, honorable, right, pure, lovely, and admirable. Think about things that are excellent and worthy of praise (Philippians 4:8).

PROBLEMS

A common misconception of life with Christ is that we're entitled to an easy life. This life is by no means easy, but we are blessed with an advantage. God said, "I have said these things to you, that in me you may have peace. In the world, you will have tribulation. But take heart, I have overcome the world (John 16:33)." God sometimes refines by allowing us to go through the fire, but we are never burned (Isaiah 43:2). Instead, we come out purified and better equipped for the purpose God set in place for us. The enemy is effective, though, at using problems to shift our perspective, ultimately hindering our vision.

When God first called Moses to lead the people of Egypt out of slavery, he did not feel qualified. He was not the best speaker and even had a stutter. He felt that this problem made him ill-equipped for the mission at hand. God responded to Moses by saying, "Who gave human beings their mouths? Who makes them deaf or mute? Who gives them sight or makes them blind? Is it not I, the Lord? Now go; I will help you speak and will teach you what to say (Exodus 4:10–12)." Our problems are not God's problems, but God's opportunities to show Himself in our situations. If Moses was the perfect orator, who would've gotten the glory for all that he did? His leadership may have been attributed to his skill set and not the supernatural power of God and what can happen when you obey the Lord's leading. God looks at our problems differently than we do. It's important that we don't get so caught in our perspective, we lose focus on the greater view and who is ultimately in control of it.

OUR PAST

The apostle Paul is one of the most influential people in Christian history. Paul was a fierce and passionate persecutor of Christians, but one encounter with Jesus Christ changed his life forever. After his conversion, that same intensity was applied to spreading the gospel. What I love most about Paul's story is that his past didn't make his message less believable, but it was a testimony of the transformative power of God through Jesus. The same is true for many of us, but we have allowed our past to bring about shame and not evidence. Shame is a result of sin, but Jesus prepaid for our sin well before we even committed it. God forgives us for our sins and transforms us from the inside out. We must also forgive ourselves and not allow our frustrations with what we've done keep us from the impact we are supposed to make today and in the future.

AMBITION

I saved the sneakiest blow to our vision for last: ambition. This attack is devious because on the surface, ambition isn't a bad thing—but it must be appropriately applied. If you're not careful, ambition can transform into something much more malicious. My Bible commentary puts it as, "Inappropriate ambition is greed in disguise." Selfish ambition is an attractive trap because the result can leave you with prestige and status, but at what expense? Ambition is healthy when applied to the advancement of the Kingdom and God's agenda, not your own. Anything else is sin and drives you further away from God.

HOW TO REATTACH

Now that we understand the ways that we get off track from the vision, let's discuss how to reposition ourselves through prayer and contentment. These two must be in your arsenal for safeguarding your vision.

PRAYER

Let's start with prayer.

James 5:16—New Living Translation

Confess your sins to each other and pray for each other so that you may be healed. The earnest prayer of a righteous person has great power and produces wonderful results.

Prayer is your method of communication with God. When you pray, you address Him with repentance, adoration, petition, and/or praise. Your prayer life allows you to address God with a level of humility that brings about clarity, even in the midst of all of the tactics of the enemy. It gives you access to intelligence and strategy from the One who has already established victory over the enemy and his devices.

How awesome is that!? Remember that I told you not to for-feit a fight that's fixed in your favor. Well, that's exactly what happens when you don't pray.

I grew up Christian, so I always knew prayer was import-ant. However, it wasn't until I was an adult that I realized the power of strategic, vehement prayer. Prayer that changed the atmosphere and induced miracles. Prayer that had transfor-mative power that only could be caused by God's response to the words of the believer. When I first quit my corporate job, I was in a very precarious position. I had taken this leap of faith that I'd wanted to do for so long, I had a clear vision of the success I wanted to achieve, but I was in this uncom-fortable gap area waiting for the vision to manifest. I didn't have money, and I was relying heavily on my then boyfriend, now husband. One morning, I woke up and heard God tell me to go and watch the movie *War Room* (2015). I was not hap-py about that instruction because, as a newly self-employed person with no money, it was not in my best interest to spend my morning watching a movie.

I decided to be obedient anyway. I enjoyed the movie, but I didn't have any major aha moments that would justify the sense of urgency behind watching the movie. After it was over, I went to the local library to check out some business and marketing books so that I could crack the code of what was going wrong in my business. As I was browsing through the business aisle, I came face-to-face with a book titled *Fer-vent*. If I'm being honest, I had no idea what that word meant, and so the book did not appeal to me until I noticed a sticker that said, "From the movie *War Room*." I instantly knew that this was no coincidence, and I immediately took the book to the register. When I got home, I read the entire thing, and my life has not been the same since. Through those pages I learned the power of prayer and how to pray strategically. As I created my own prayer closet and used that book as my guide to pray fervently for every area of my life, including businesses, little-by-little, things began to change. I woke up that day looking for the worldly answer to my problems, and I got the true resolution to winning in life: prayer.

Friend—without prayer, you will not achieve total life success God's way. How will you know His way if you don't communicate with Him? How will you remind yourself—and the devil—that you are not to be played with and you are relentless about seeing the vision through, even if it seems like an uphill battle? You must pray without ceasing (1 Thessalonians 5:16–18).

I have included on the next page a chart of the different names of God. Calling God by the name that reflects who I need Him to be or am thanking Him for in that moment has helped me tremendously in prayer. Not that God needs to be reminded, but sometimes I need to be reminded that He is Yahweh Shalom when I need peace and that He's Yahweh Rapha when I need healing. Use this as a reference point as you grow in your own prayer life.

NAME	MEANING	REFERENCE
Elohim	God	Genesis 1:1, Numbers 23:19, Psalm 19:1
Yahweh	The Lord	Genesis 2:4, Exodus 6:2,3
El Elyon	God Most High	Genesis 14:17–20, Numbers 24:16, Psalm 7:17, Isaiah 14:13,14
El Roi	God Who Sees	Genesis 16:13
El Shaddai	God Almighty	Genesis 17:1, Psalm 91:1
Yahweh Jireh	The Lord Will Provide	Genesis 22:13,14
Yahweh Nissi	The Lord Is My Banner	Exodus 17:5
Jehovah-Rapha	The Lord Who Heals	Exodus 15:26, Psalm 41:3, Jonah 2:5–7, Psalm 23:3, Psalm 147:3, John 14:27
Adonai	Lord	Deuteronomy 6:4
Yahweh Elohe Yisrael	The Lord of Israel	Judges 5:3, Psalm 59:5, Isaiah 17:6, Zephaniah 2:9
Yahweh Shalom	The Lord Is Peace	Judges 6:24
Qedosh Yisrael	Holy One of Israel	Isaiah 1:4
Yahweh Sabaoth	Lord of Hosts	1 Samuel 1:3, Isaiah 6:1–3

El Olam	Everlasting God	Isaiah 40:28–31
Yahweh Tsid-kenu	The Lord Is Our Righ-teousness	Jeremiah 23:6; 33:16
Yahweh Sham-mah	The Lord Is There	Ezekiel 48:35
Attiq Yomin	Ancient of Days	Daniel 7:9,13

CONTENTMENT

Psalm 13—New Living Translation

For the choir director: A psalm of David.
O Lord, how long will you forget me? Forever?
How long will you look the other way?
How long must I struggle with anguish in my soul,
with sorrow in my heart every day?
How long will my enemy have the upper hand?

Turn and answer me, O Lord my God!
Restore the sparkle to my eyes, or I will die.
Don't let my enemies gloat, saying, "We have defeated him!"
Don't let them rejoice at my downfall.

But I trust in your unfailing love.
I will rejoice because you have rescued me.

I will sing to the Lord
because he is good to me.

Prayer brings about contentment. When you are content, you see clearly and are not fazed by the enemy's devices. I love the that psalm of David because he starts his prayer frustrated, anxious, and unsatisfied with how long God was taking. His problems seemed big, and God's presence, amid the problem, seemed small. David opened the lines of communication through prayer and expressed to God how he felt. By the end, he did a 180-degree turn. He went from mourning to rejoicing—complaining about where God was to singing to Him and proclaiming His goodness. When you pray, your perspective changes, and you're brought from your reality to God's reality.

Vision is crucial, naturally and spiritually, so we must protect it at all costs. To be uncompromising is to be relentless in pursuit of the big picture. To do that, the picture must be clear. We have an adversary who wants our destination to be blurry and our commitment to fade, but we must not grow weary or get impatient with our journey and continue to fight the good fight of faith.

CHAPTER 6

MULTIPLYING VS. MULTITASKING

Romans 12:2—New Living Translation

Don't copy the behavior and customs of this world, but let God transform you into a new person by changing the way you think. Then you will learn to know God's will for you, which is good and pleasing and perfect.

I hope by now you've fully grasped the overarching theme of this book: Live by faith and be uncompromising. Before we get into the system I've created for you to do this and achieve the balanced life you desire, we must first address the mindset. In order to see the vision through, you have to have your mind right. I believe that one of the keys to a successful life is to operate in wisdom. Wisdom elevates your mind and emotions, which then govern your behavior to operate intelligently with good judgment and insight. Let's dive a little deeper into what wisdom is and why it's important.

WISDOM IS APPLIED TRUTH

A wise person is marked by deep understanding, keen discernment, and a capacity for sound judgment. The benefits include a long, satisfying life, favor with God and people, success, health, peace, protection, God's approval, riches, honor, etc. Wisdom is a legacy that will live far beyond anything material. I recently attended the funeral of a relative of a family friend. Each person who got up and spoke had a different lesson or nugget of knowledge that the deceased shared with them.

I couldn't tell you anything about the assets or finances that were left behind, but the impact of the wealth of knowledge passed down is what I hope to leave for my family. The book of Proverbs is known as the book of wisdom. It teaches readers how to live a disciplined, sensible life and how to do what is just. It's a guide of moral instruction. Proverbs was written mostly by Solomon, who was heavily influenced by his father, David. David's wisdom was passed down to his son, and then his son, further transferring the wisdom to all of us, who can read it today.

Wisdom is how we're going to build a life we don't need a vacation from. It's going to be the foundation, coupled with our faith, of us being virtuous and efficient women. The prototype of a dynamic woman can be found in Proverbs 31. She has no name, but she is so virtuous and powerful that she doesn't even need one. Whenever I feel like I'm hitting a brick wall with being adept in managing my life, I always revisit this chapter. It never ceases to amaze me how you can read something a million times but every time you get something different. The last time I studied her, I read the text line by line. I looked up definitions of every word and sought out commentary from multiple Bible study sources to make sure no message went unrealized. While doing this, I got the mind-blowing revelation that a powerful woman is a multiplier versus a multitasker.

Multitasking seems efficient on the surface because you're accomplishing multiple things in a limited window of time. Where the problem comes in, though, is that the quality of what you're getting done is not the same as it would be if you were focused. What's really happening when you multitask is you're shifting attention from one thing to the next. You may go from email to music to chat alerts to Instagram to Facebook to whatever every few seconds, but you're never really being fully present at anything. Studies show that heavy multitaskers were less mentally organized, struggled switching from one task to another, and had a tough time differentiating relevant from irrelevant details. Research also found that balance in more than one task at a time hinders employee performance. So much so that multitasking has an ultimate financial cost of $450 million per year globally.

Now let's discuss multiplying . . .

Matthew 25:14–30—New Living Translation

Again, the Kingdom of Heaven can be illustrated by the story of a man going on a long trip. He called together his servants and entrusted his money to them while he was gone. He gave five bags of silver to one, two bags of silver to another, and one bag of silver to the last— dividing it in proportion to their abilities. He then left on his trip. The servant who received the five bags of silver began to invest the money and earned five more. The servant with two bags of silver also went to work and earned two more. But the servant who received the one bag of silver dug a hole in the ground and hid the master's money. After a long time, their master returned from his trip and called them to give an account of how they had used his money.

The servant to whom he had entrusted the five bags of silver came forward with five more and said, "Master, you gave me five bags of silver to invest, and I have earned five more." The master was full of praise. "Well done, my good and faithful servant. You have been faithful in handling this small amount, so now I will give you many more responsibilities. Let's celebrate together!" The servant who had received the two bags of silver came forward and said, "Master, you gave me two bags of silver to invest, and I have earned two more." The master said, "Well done, my good and faithful servant. You have been faithful in handling this small amount, so now I will give you many more responsibilities. Let's celebrate together!"

Then the servant with the one bag of silver came and said, "Master, I knew you were a harsh man, harvesting crops you didn't plant and gathering crops you didn't cultivate.

I was afraid I would lose your money, so I hid it in the earth. Look, here is your money back." But the master replied, "You wicked and lazy servant! If you knew I harvested crops I didn't plant and gathered crops I didn't cultivate, why didn't you deposit my money in the bank? At least I could have gotten some interest on it." Then he ordered, "Take the money from this servant, and give it to the one with the ten bags of silver. To those who use what they are given, even more will be given, and they will have an abundance. But from those who do nothing, even what little they have will be taken away. Now throw this useless servant into outer darkness, where there will be weeping and gnashing of teeth."

The preceding text is also referred to as the "parable of talents" in other translations, but no matter what version you read, the message is the same: We are to take what God gave us and multiply it. In the parable, the master praised those who multiplied and then blessed them with more. For the one who buried his gift, it was taken away and he was scolded. What are you doing with the gift that God has given you? Are you multiplying it or burying it? There was a time that I was so frustrated with God because I didn't know what my gift was. I had many skills, but I was confused about what my God-given gift was that I was supposed to use to make an impact.

I heard an answer so clearly: speaking. If I'm being honest, I was a bit disappointed with this answer. I wanted some long, elaborate answer that brought about this miraculous revelation, but that's not what I got. The answer, speaking, felt too simple. But it felt simple because a gift never seems as miraculous as it is to the person who embodies it. Similar to someone who can sing. Their voice may bring the hardest individual to tears, but to them, it's just their voice. It's not spectacular to them because they live with it; they've always lived with it. Same for me: I didn't consider speaking a gift, because I didn't have to do anything extra to be able to communicate. I just opened my mouth.

I was reminded of my senior year in high school when I was running for homecoming queen. To win, you had to campaign, participate in a pageant where your scores went to the ultimate vote, and then the students voted as well. The pageant consisted of a question-and-answer segment, and I received perfect scores across the board from the judges. After the pageant, parents and teachers would come up to me and compliment me on my ability to articulate myself. Even earlier than that, I remember being ten years old at dinner with my parents and my brother. I was telling my parents about my favorite show at the time, *Kim Possible*, and the episode I watched that day. The waitress overheard our conversation and told my parents that I was very articulate for my age.

When I was in college, I took a speech class, and one day I was super late to class. As I was walking in, the professor was informing the class that we were getting ready to begin our midterm and were required to write an impromptu speech on the subject assigned to us. We had ten minutes to research the topic, make our points, and then present in front of the class. I was sweating bullets because I did not know how I was going to deliver without any real time to prepare. I ended up getting the topic of "censorship," and time started ticking. I don't remember any of the points I made, but I remember that I had the attention of my peers throughout the entire speech. No one talking to each other and no one was looking at their phones. Everyone was engaged and locked in. I used a hand gesture in my speech where I covered my mouth when I used the word censorship, and, by the end, the audience was doing the gesture with me. I got an A on that midterm and lots of kudos from my classmates and the professor, who enjoyed the speech.

When praying about my gift and hearing the word "speaking," I revisited all these memories. Now that I knew what my gift was, it was time for me to multiply it. I have been able to take this gift of speaking and turn it into a successful podcast, speaking business, books, and other print products. That's four sources of income from one gift. You don't have to have a million gifts; you just have to multiply what God has blessed you with.

Ask yourself, "How can you take what you have and multiply it?"

Here's a super simple, three-step way to start:

1. Identify your gift
2. List the different formats in which you can present your gift to the world
3. Make them profitable

Example:

IDENTIFY YOUR GIFT	COOKING
List the different formats in which you can present your gift to the world	1. Catering/Private Chef 2. Cookbook with top recipes 3. Online brand showcasing food tutorials
Make them profitable	1. Charge for catering/chef services 2. Sell cookbook online and in retailers 3. Create sponsored videos for advertisers

As you can see, you don't have to be a jack-of-all-trades to be a multiplier. You can be a master of one and then present that one in multiple ways.

Multiplying doesn't just apply to your gift or your business. It's also applicable to daily decisions. The root is to make sure that everywhere you spend your time and effort, you are getting as much of a return as possible with that energy.

MAKING THE SHIFT

Now how do we move from multitasking to multiplying? It's simple, we focus. When you focus, you are able to see clearly. You're no longer mindlessly doing a bunch of things at the same time for the sake of getting them done. Instead, you are zeroing in on a task, ensuring that it is complete in a way that is of quality and has a return on the effort being put forth. Focus unlocks intentionality, and with this you're more deliberate in what you do, making you more effective. You see, the life we want that's full of peace and harmony and free of overwhelm and imbalance isn't some foreign place that's impossible to get to. It's actually right where you are, able to be achieved by simply being more focused and intentional. The Proverbs 31 woman embodied two essential characteristics that I believe will assist us in making the shift to being a multiplier:

SHE PREPARED AND DELEGATED

Proverbs 31:15—New Living Translation

She gets up before dawn to prepare breakfast for her household and plan the day's work for her servant girls.

In order to have it all, you do not have to do it all. It's not a badge of honor to be stretched thin and overworked. The superwoman complex has left many women unfulfilled and exhausted for far too long. We'll dive deeper into the best way to delegate in the next chapter, but for now I want you to divorce yourself from the train of thought that you must do everything.

SHE INSPECTED AND INVESTED IN WHAT HAD A RETURN

Proverbs 31:16–18—New Living Translation

She goes to inspect a field and buys it;
with her earnings she plants a vineyard.
She is energetic and strong,
a hard worker.
She makes sure her dealings are profitable;
her lamp burns late into the night.

When you inspect something, you assess its condition before acquiring it. This lets me know that we must be intentional about what we take ownership of. Before committing to a task, project, or any type of request that will require your time and energy, inspect it first. We must not make decisions out of emotions or without thought. Our time, energy, and resources are valuable, so where we spend them, we want to make sure we're getting a return on our investment. Something I've learned after stepping into a new role as a parent is just how valuable my time and resources are. Every "yes" I give is saying "no" to something else. Before I give that "yes," I must inspect and evaluate if it's worth it. Same for you. What are your "yeses" saying "no" to? Is it worth it? Making the shift from multitasker to multiplier doesn't happen overnight. It happens one decision and one commitment at a time.

Now that we understand why and how to shift from multitasker to multiplier, let's get into the system that I believe is going to upgrade your life and your effectiveness forever.

CHAPTER 7

THE PILLARS OF TOTAL LIFE MASTERY

It's time for us to switch gears and focus specifically on what you need to do to experience harmony in your life. Up until this point, we have debunked the dos and don'ts of being uncompromising and achieving total life success.

Let's recap:

DO	DON'T
• Live by faith	• Settle
• Be obedient	• Give into perfectionism
• Multiply your efforts	• Multitask
• Protect your vision	• Give into your emotions, fear, or anxiety

It's important to note that I believe that there is a difference between total life mastery and total life success. Success isn't accidental but rather a result of a series of actions that got you to that point. Those actions are where the *mastery* aspect comes in. When you master something, you become adept at that particular thing. It's now a skill or a proficiency. I am successful at creating influential podcasts because I have mastered how to reach and foster an active community via that medium. The skill didn't come overnight or by accident. It was a result of developing, testing—and testing again—a system over time.

That's what we're going to do in this chapter and the next—lay the foundation for a system that will allow you to be skilled at managing the many aspects of your life efficiently. Before we get to that though, let's discuss the pillars that will hold that foundation together. These pillars are essential. If one is removed, you risk everything falling apart. The pillars are purpose, faith, discipline, wellness, and strategy.

PURPOSE

Our ultimate purpose is to be like Christ, obey God, and live a set-apart life. We are to be salt and light (Matthew 5:13–16). Many times, we make the mistake of making a purpose about us and not about God, and that won't work. Mastering your life is about mastering yourself, and that means keeping your ambition and desires secondary to Him and His will. This doesn't mean that what you want doesn't matter, because He will give you the desires of your heart (Psalm 37:4). But those desires cannot be first. We can't serve two masters.

If you start from the beginning of the Word, the fall of mankind always followed a priority shift in the people. They shifted from obeying God to giving into their selfish desires. Losing sight of purpose will do the same for you. I don't want that for you. I want you to have life and have it abundantly (John 10:10). I want you to experience blessings everywhere you look and everywhere you go (Amos 9:13–15). This is a life that is promised to you by God, but to receive and maintain it, your purpose must be clear.

With purpose comes faith, and that's the pillar we will discuss next.

FAITH

Hebrews 11:1—New International Version

Now faith is confidence in what we hope for and assurance about what we do not see.

Everything we talked about until now has been about faith. Without faith, none of this matters. I love the definition of faith in the preceding text, mostly because of the first word: now. Your faith has to be current. You can't build the life of your dreams on your mother's faith, your grandmother's faith, or even the faith of your past seasons that got you to where you are today. Your faith has to be present. You must decide every day that you're going to build what you may not even have the capacity to fully understand, simply because God said so.

Let's review some examples of faith that we haven't discussed yet:

GIDEON

Judges 6:15–16—New International Version

"Pardon me, my lord," Gideon replied, "but how can I save Israel? My clan is the weakest in Manasseh, and I am the least in my family." The Lord answered, "I will be with you, and you will strike down all the Midianites, leaving none alive."

What's interesting to me about Gideon is that his faith took a lot of convincing to get to. He asked God for many signs and miracles before he acted on the instructions he was given. He had an unfathomable task at hand (defeating a powerful army of over one hundred thousand men with only a group of three hundred) and he was in a space where nothing about his circumstances showed that God was with him. Have you found yourself in that position? Unable to have faith in the next because God seems absent in the now? This is an effective tactic of the enemy to fuel our disbelief. The enemy wants us to think that it's God's fault that we're in the predicament that we're in and it's useless to keep trying to do things His way. But that's a lie.

Gideon was in the middle of the consequences of the Israelites' evil actions where God handed them over to the Midianites for seven years. A little accountability and self-awareness would've revealed to him that his circumstances weren't an indicator of the absence of God but rather a direct reflection of bad decisions. Same with us. We can't blame God for holes we've dug for ourselves. Instead, we must repent and recommit to His agenda. God is with us, even in the midst of the consequences of our own actions. Even though Gideon was ultimately obedient, his obedience was delayed because he met God with his humanity and not his faith. He asked God to prove and confirm multiple times before he followed his instructions.

God was gracious with Gideon by agreeing to his many requests of confirmation, but we don't know how many chances He will give us so we must obey Him now. We must approach every day leading with our faith and not our humanity. God will be with you as you go out to complete impossible tasks in His name. The task has to seem impossible so people know it's God. The impossibility of the test is the foundation of a powerful testimony. This is why this pillar is so important. Let your commitment to God be bigger than your fear of "what if it doesn't work out." Don't delay the miracle by leading your days with disbelief.

RAHAB

Hebrews 11:31—New Living Translation

It was by faith that Rahab the prostitute was not destroyed with the people in her city who refused to obey God. For she had given a friendly welcome to the spies.

Rahab was only one of two women who are listed as great examples of faith in Hebrews 11. She was a prostitute and a Canaanite who put her life on the line for a God she didn't know, which ended up saving her life. Rahab hid the spies that Moses sent over to scout out Jericho. Even when the Canaanite king came and asked her where they were, she lied and said that they left and she didn't know where they went (Joshua 2:4–7). After the king left, she went to where the spies were hiding and told them that she knew that the Lord had given them the land (Joshua 2:8) and asked that they return her favor by protecting her and her family. She feared for her life because she knew the consequences of what she was doing, but she didn't let fear keep her from the faith she had that God would protect her. And God delivered. Is there a lingering fear that you have about God if He is going to deliver on His promises to you? Is it keeping you from acting in faith? Use Rahab's story as an example of how to act in faith despite of fear.

ELIZABETH

Luke 1:43–45—New Living Translation

"Why am I so honored that the mother of my Lord should visit me? When I heard your greeting, the baby in my womb jumped for joy. You are blessed because you believed that the Lord would do what he said."

Elizabeth's story of faith is one that I hold dear to my heart. Her story of faith fueled my own as I waited for God to fulfill His promise to me of having a child. Elizabeth was an older woman who was barren. Back in those days, this was especially shameful, but Elizabeth didn't waver in her faith. Elizabeth and her husband, Zechariah, were both righteous in God's eyes (Luke 1:6).

But even in their faithfulness, they still hadn't received the child they were praying for and were both in old age. When the angel of the Lord told them that not only will they have a son, John the Baptist, but that he will be a man with the spirit and power of Elijah and make room for the Messiah, they responded in two different ways. Zechariah responded with doubt, which made the angel completely mute him so that he couldn't speak against what God was doing. However, Elizabeth responded with faith and immediately went into praise. Elizabeth's story shows us that God doesn't forget those who are faithful to Him. Sometimes we put our own timelines and expectations on when and how we want God to bless us, but He isn't obligated to—and usually doesn't—

conform to our expectations. As you work to keep your faith current, release your expectations of how you want God to show up. Instead, surrender to not just His will, but His ways.

In these examples of Faith, I want you to see yourself in the humanity of these individuals and notice their decision to act in faith despite it. The Bible says that faith comes by hearing, that is, hearing the Good News about Christ (Romans 10:17). Use these examples to solidify this pillar of faith in your life.

EXERCISING YOUR FAITH

I believe that faith grows as you exercise it, and you can either feed it and make it stronger or starve it and make it weak. The point of this pillar is to create a life in which you're constantly in a position to fuel your faith. Because as your faith grows and gets stronger, so does your confidence about this life you're building. You stop seeing your life through the lens of what you're capable of and begin to see through a lens through which everything is possible because you're doing it with Him.

I love to exercise my faith by being present in the miracles that happen around me every day. In earlier chapters, I told you about my history of miscarriages and my desperation for God to bless me with a child. I didn't know that God would continue to build my faith muscle by seeing me through multiple health challenges after giving birth. When I gave birth to my son, it seemed as if trauma came one thing after the other. Towards the end of my pregnancy, I developed gestational hypertension. I was in the home stretch, and my doctor told me that if I didn't go into labor naturally, I would have to get induced in a week. I wasn't happy about the news, but I was willing to do anything to keep myself and my baby safe. I ended up getting induced, but my son was not cooperating. Even today, my son is very strong-willed and does not like to be coerced into doing something he doesn't want to do. I ended up bringing my baby boy into the world via Caesarean section.

Later that evening, I developed a fever and a very rapid heart rate, which the medical team had a hard time diagnosing. I just had a major surgery, my hormones were all over the place, I was trying to breastfeed, and my husband had a look of worry and fear on his face that I'd never seen before. I remember getting to a point where I was so frustrated, scared, and mentally foggy that I told everyone to leave me alone for a minute. I staggered to the bathroom with my IV, shut the door, and prayed. I began to recite every scripture of healing I could paraphrase. I cried out to God, and I said, "Jesus," repeatedly until the nurse came in and told me I needed to lie down. I didn't have time at that moment to cave. I needed to exercise the same faith that got me to the delivery room in order to get home healthy. They ended up giving me antibiotics and treating what was happening as an infection. After a few days, we were all able to go home.

My faith muscle needed to be exercised once again just a couple of days after returning home. One morning, I woke up and one of my feet was three times its normal size. It wasn't the usual pregnancy or postpartum swelling; it was huge, and I barely got my shoe over it. I decided to take my blood pressure, and it was very high. I called the nurses station, and they told me that swelling was normal and to just sit down and put my feet up. With the maternal mortality rate for black women so high, I knew throughout this whole journey that I was going to advocate for myself and not let anyone downplay my concerns. I told the nurse that the swelling I was experiencing was not normal and that my blood pressure was high. She tried to assure me that I was fine, but I insisted that she put a doctor on the phone and told her that even if she said I was fine, I would be showing up to be evaluated. She put me on hold, spoke to a doctor, and told me to return to labor and delivery to be evaluated. I ended up getting admitted and diagnosed with postpartum preeclampsia, a condition that takes the lives of many women every year.

If I didn't advocate for myself, it could've progressed and taken my life as well. While in the hospital again, this time without my husband or newborn son, I found myself back in the bathroom, pleading with God for my life. I brought my Bible with me, and I read scripture after scripture about healing. I spoke life over myself, and I prayed over the room, the doctors, nurses, and anyone who would play a part in my care. After a few days, I went back home on blood pressure medication to keep my pressure down. When I got home, I set my mind to being off of the medication. Through diet, exercise, and taking supplements, I was able to get off of the blood pressure medicine within four months. My pressure has been normal ever since. My journey to motherhood is a miracle that God performed for me that intensifies my faith. It's hard not to trust and be confident when my life—my health—is a testimony to God's faithfulness.

MIRACLE MARY

Miracle Mary is my grandmother. Earlier this year, she was diagnosed with stage four anaplastic thyroid cancer. This diagnosis came with a prognosis of three months. I watched my grandmother go from being healthy, completely independent, and living on her own to being told she had a very rare and aggressive cancer that spread all over her body. We had no idea where the cancer came from, how long it had been in her body, or why there were no signs of it before. What we thought would be a quick office visit turned into her going to the hospital immediately. Shortly after, she was bound to a walker, given oxygen, and needed around-the-clock care.

I watched the strongest person I knew become sick overnight. I am who I am because of my grandmother and her prayers. And during this time, I took it upon myself to be on my hands and knees, praying for her. And then a miracle unfolded. Day by day, she started to get stronger. Her doctors were astounded by how well she was doing, despite the diagnosis. Within a month or two, she no longer needed oxygen, was able to walk on her own, and was just as she was before the cancer. Her tumors began to shrink and she earned the new name Miracle Mary. Those three months that they give patients with this type of cancer came and went. I watched God totally restore her and give her and me a testimony to share about His healing power. My own journey and watching Miracle Mary invigorate me. They reinforce the pillar of faith in my life as I go about the path God has laid out for me.

Is your faith strengthened yet? As you take this journey of total life success, I can't emphasize enough that you're doing all of the things, wearing all these hats, so that He can be glorified and pleased. And it's impossible to please God without faith (Hebrews 11:6).

DISCIPLINE

Proverbs 1:7—New Living Translation

Fear of the Lord is the foundation of true knowledge, but fools despise wisdom and discipline.

Discipline covers two different grounds: discipline in the form of correction from the Lord, as well as discipline in self-control over one's actions and decisions. God is the alpha and omega. He is omnipresent and omniscient. As humans, we can only conceptualize what we see and have the capacity to understand. God has a bird's-eye view and knowledge on how everything is going to work out. He knows the plans He has for us, and He lays out a path so that we follow those plans. Our humanity, though, can sometimes get us off track, and that's why we must be open and receptive to the loving discipline of God that corrects us and steers us back into the right direction. It's His correcting discipline that creates the self-control in us necessary to see out His purposes and plans.

This is similar to how you discipline your own children. I have a toddler now, and he is definitely living up to the toddler reputation. One of his favorite things to attempt is put his fingers into the outlets. He doesn't know the danger in what he's doing because he doesn't have that knowledge. He just knows that he believes placing his fingers in the outlets is what he wants to do. When he first started doing this, we had to correct him so that he understood that what he was doing was not good for him. Now—whenever he is around an outlet—I can tell he is thinking about putting his fingers in, but he pauses and exercises self-control to decide against it. It's the same with God and us: discipline creates discipline (self-control). Remember, mastering your life is about mastering yourself, and that happens through discipline.

WELLNESS

3 John 2—The Passion Translation

Beloved friend, I pray that you are prospering in every way and that you continually enjoy good health, just as your soul is prospering.

I truly believe that health is wealth. Our bodies are luxury vehicles that require premium fuel to run. We live in a vanity world where people are obsessed with the physical appearance of their bodies, but that's not what I'm talking about here. When referring to wellness, I mean your insides should be powered through nutrition and physical activity to be able to support what God has called you to do. You need the mental clarity to show up sharp, focused and alert, each day. This is accomplished through your wellness regime.

My birth and postpartum experiences highlighted to me how important health and wellness are and the severity of the consequences when we don't take care of ourselves. After I was released from the hospital the second time, I made a request to God to be taken off the blood pressure medication and promised that I would better take care of the body He gave me. We only get one. I started to do a deep dive into researching supplements, products, and natural remedies that I could incorporate into my life to assist my body in operating at its best. My hard work paid off when my husband and I decided to take out new life insurance policies. I was dreading the physical exam because of all I had gone through.

I was beating myself up because not only did my poor choices lead to my birth challenges, but they'd now led to a crappy policy that would take away from the benefits I was looking to leave my children. To my surprise, the results of my physical came back excellent, and I was approved for the best policy the company had to offer. So not only will my children be taken care of when I pass, but there are benefits available that we can use while I'm living. Looking at my policy and at the amount of bills that piled up due to my hospital stay, I was clearly able to see that health is an asset and sickness is a liability.

Wellness is not just physical, but it's mental as well. According to the report *The State of Mental Health in America* by Mental Health America (MHA):

- In 2017-2018, 19 percent of adults experienced a mental illness—an increase of 1.5 million people over the previous year's dataset.

- Suicidal ideation among adults is increasing. The percentage of adults in the U.S. who are experiencing serious thoughts of suicide increased 0.15 percent from 2016-2017 to 2017-2018—an additional 460,000 people.

A good friend of mine always says that she believes every person should have a therapist, and I couldn't agree more. Your mental health matters. Even as a person of faith, your mental health matters, and therapy should be part of your wellness regime. You can pray and go to therapy. You can love Jesus and see a licensed therapist. I've been in therapy or counseling multiple times, and the practical tools I learned are things I still use today to be proactive about my mental wellness.

Friend, are you taking care of yourself, both physically and mentally? If the answer is no, I want to take a moment to think about ways you better fuel and take care of your mind and body.

STRATEGY

You can be saved and strategic.

I have come across so many women who are either so saved that they're not earthly good, or they're so strategic that there's no room for God to move in their rigid plan. The sweet spot is to keep God in His rightful place—to be flexible to move as He leads you—but also have a systemized plan so that you can be intentional about what you want to accomplish. My meltdown moment at my white board after having my son was my lack of strategy blowing up in my face. I knew moving forward that I needed to create a game plan that was going to keep me from ever being in that place today. That blueprint is what we'll be working through in the next chapter.

CHAPTER 8

THE BLUEPRINT

Now that we know the pillars that support the blueprint, let's craft the blueprint itself. In this chapter, we're going to get to work. We've spent every chapter up until this point preparing mentally, emotionally, and spiritually for the system that you will create and implement to master your life. The blueprint is broken down into four phases: census, layout, execution, and accountability. Over the next few pages, we will work through each phase together to craft your ultimate plan to total life success.

PHASE 1: CENSUS

We can't begin to craft a plan without taking into account where we are. In this phase, you will evaluate your goals, priorities, your current time management habits, and what you need to adjust in order to be more productive and effective.

WHAT DO YOU DESIRE?

Psalm 37:4—New International Version

Take delight in the Lord, and he will give you the desires of your heart.

Use the space below to write out what you want in both the short-term and long-term. This isn't the place to be modest but rather a place to be bold. The Bible says that He will do exceedingly and abundantly above anything that we could ask for or think (Ephesians 3:20). Make this list with the understanding that no matter how big it is to you, it's still easy to God.

_____

_____

_____

_____

_____

_____

_____

_____

_____

_____

_____

_____

_____

_____

_____

_____

WHAT ARE YOUR PRIORITIES?

I want you to identify your top priorities and list them in order of importance below.

———————————————————————————————
———————————————————————————————
———————————————————————————————
———————————————————————————————
———————————————————————————————
———————————————————————————————
———————————————————————————————
———————————————————————————————
———————————————————————————————

TAKE INVENTORY

What's on your plate? Use the space below to take inventory of all the things you spend any amount of time on at the moment. Even things that seem to be small or seemingly insignificant, if they require even a minute of your time, write them down. Moving forward, I'm going to refer to any roles you have (mother, wife, job, business, caregiver, etc.) as "hats."

———————————————————————————————
———————————————————————————————
———————————————————————————————
———————————————————————————————
———————————————————————————————
———————————————————————————————

Now, for the next seven days, I want you to use a timer to measure how much time you spend on each thing. If you find yourself doing things during the week that aren't listed, add them and time them as well. Once you have the time, add it in parentheses next to the item.

Did you include time for yourself on your plate? Time where you can finally rest as a human-being and not a human-doing? If the answer is no, add that in there and make it a priority :-)

EVALUATE

As you evaluate your findings, think about the following:

1. Is there any time being wasted? Have you noticed any time wasters you wrote down, like scrolling on social media for an hour before you get out of the bed? Or talking to your bestie for two hours on the phone in the middle of the day? Whatever your time wasters are, go back to the plate and cross them off. Add up the total amount of time spent, and write it where it says, "time found."

2. Can anything be delegated? Friend, in order to have it all, you most certainly don't have to do it all. Sometimes we bite off more than we can chew, and we need to spit it back out. Your time should be spent on what only you

can do. Chores like laundry, house cleaning, and grocery shopping can all be hired out in some way. Add up the time that you spend on each of these chores and add that number where you have "time found."

3. Does where you're spending time align with your priorities? There is an adage that says, "If you want to see what a person values, look at where they spend their money." I believe the same for time. I can tell you what your priorities are by looking at where you spend the most time. The purpose of this exercise is to make sure what you do aligns with what you say you want. Many women lack harmony in their lives not because they want to, but because they fail to recognize when their time isn't being well-budgeted. This is a phase that you may need to revisit more than once, especially as your life evolves. If you have another child, if your business grows, if you take on a new role, etc., you need to revisit this phase so that you can always have your thumb on the pulse of what's going on in your life and how you're going to create boundaries and routines that support the accomplishment of your goals and attention to your priorities.

I understand that delegating certain chores costs money and not everyone has the means to do that, but even if you're not able to do it financially, I want you to see how much time you will have back if you did. Let this serve as motivation to find the means to make it happen. Do you need to charge more in your business to accommodate? Can you cut back on Starbucks for a month to get that housekeeper? Can you eat out less to allocate funds for the laundry service? Maybe you only hire the housekeeper once a month to do a deep cleaning and spend your time maintaining in between. This saves money and still gives you some of your time back. There's always a way to make it happen, but use this opportunity to see how much time you will save by delegating tasks that don't require you to be the one to do them.

PHASE 2: LAYOUT

Now that you understand where you are, it's time to create the plan to define where you're going. In this phase we will learn the key elements every success system needs and craft an overall schedule that allows you to effectively take care of yourself and manage the hats you wear.

PROTECT YOUR PRIORITIES

As you lay out what your new schedule is going to look like, it's important to start by protecting your priorities. If you don't, your time will control you and you won't control your time. We all have a budget of twenty-four hours in a day, and it's our job to use that budget wisely and strategically. The best way to protect your priorities is to create boundaries and, more importantly, enforce those boundaries. If having dinner with your family is important to you, create a boundary around when your work day ends and stick to it.

When my grandmother first got sick, I spent a lot of time feeling like my day was running me. I was juggling my household, helping to care for her, promoting my business, and the list goes on. I was mentally and physically drained, and I felt like because I had so much going on, I was failing on all fronts—especially as a mother. I was running around so much that I felt as if I was not giving my son the time he needed. When I revisited this system for myself, I realized that I had my son listed as a priority—but where most of my time was going told a different story. I had to go back to the drawing board and protect my priorities. I was stretched thin because I allowed myself to get to that point, and that needed to change. I created a new rule that it was nonnegotiable that I spent time with my son in the morning when he woke up and in the evening before he went to bed. I stopped taking meetings in the evening. Even if I was tending to my extended family, everyone knew I needed to be home by six in the evening and was not available before nine in the morning.

This one boundary instantly gave me peace of mind. Now, instead of feeling stretched thin, I felt in control of my day and that I was giving my best to the people and things that mattered most to me.

REST + ROUTINE

Studies show that resting improves your mental health, reduces stress, improves your mood, and the list goes on. Rest must be on your priority list when you're building the blueprint for your life. When creating your schedule, plan for at least eight hours of sleep at night. Depending on your job or business, you may also need to schedule some time to rest during the day. It could be a nap or a simple mental break for a moment to rest your mind. Someone like a therapist may need breaks between clients to decompress. A professor may need a break between lectures to gather their thoughts. When I'm in strategist mode, and I am working with clients during the day on their podcasts and businesses, I often need to schedule a break and limit the amount of people I talk to in a day. If I don't put those controls in place, I get a headache and feel extremely drained because I've poured out so much. Whatever breaks you need, take them. This plan won't work if you're not operating at your best and if you're not fully rested.

AM ROUTINE

Your morning routine is an opportunity to start your day in a space where you're joyful, mentally clear, and ready to be productive. Gone are the days where we roll over and check our phones, emails, and texts. When you start your day that way, you're starting the day in a reactive way as opposed to proactive. You have peace when you're proactive. I want you to craft a morning routine for yourself that takes care of your priorities and allows you to start your day peacefully. It doesn't have to be long, but it has to be intentional. Since you're a woman of faith, I suggest having your time with God in the morning. What that looks like is totally up to you.

When the weather permits, my favorite morning routine is to wake up before my family and go for a prayer walk. I usually do about three miles, and I listen to gospel music, pray, and listen. I take time to breathe the fresh air, look at the beautiful flowers, and smile and say hello to people out walking their dogs. It's amazing. Not only am I getting my body up and moving, which is great for my physical health, but I am setting the tone for my day with peace and joy. If my family is still asleep when I get home, I make a cup of coffee and just sit down and enjoy it. I smell the hazelnut creamer, taste the coffee, and enjoy the warmth of the mug. It's so simple but so serene. It's a total difference from when I let my toddler be my alarm clock and I start my day at his disposal, or when I have to put my coffee in the microwave ten times before I ever even finish it.

What's going to be your morning routine? Write some ideas below.

_____

_____

_____

_____

_____

_____

_____

_____

_____

_____

_____

_____

After you write your ideas, take each one and try it for a week to see which one you like the best. If you like more than one, that's awesome—now you have variety. It's also important to time yourself as you do them. You want to know how long it takes you to do, so that you can schedule the appropriate amount of time for it.

PM ROUTINE

After the kids are asleep and you're ready to go to bed, do you have a routine? Or do you just hop in the bed with your phone and check your emails, texts, and social media? I'm guilty of the latter. There was a period of time where I was getting horrible sleep. I would sleep at night with a headache, dream about whatever email I was answering or business task I let myself work on, and then wake up with a headache with no feeling of being rested. It was terrible. I spent my days groggy and taking Tylenol. I ended up talking to someone about it, and they instructed me to create a bedtime routine and to set better boundaries around my bedtime. I already had a rule that I didn't work between 4:30 in the afternoon and 7:00 in the evening, because I spend that time with my family; but I had a bad habit of opening my laptop back up when my son was asleep.

I created a new rule that I don't work after 8:00 at night, and my phone goes on do not disturb. Now that I established these new boundaries, it was time to craft my bedtime routine. My routine consisted of taking a shower with a body wash that contained scents like lavender, eucalyptus, or anything that helped me relax. When doing my skincare regime, I washed my face and let the warm washcloth just sit for a moment and enjoyed that warmth on my face for a moment. Then, I made a cup of chamomile tea and lay in bed with my husband. My routine was simple, but the result was much better sleep, no more headaches, and a rested feeling the next morning.

What's going to be your bedtime routine? Write some ideas below.

_____

_____

_____

_____

_____

_____

_____

_____

_____

_____

_____

After you write your ideas, take each one and try it for a week as you did with the AM routine.

YOUR HAPPY LIST

In addition to resting at night, make time during the day and week to refuel by pouring back into yourself. When I first had my son, I was mentally all over the place. I was experiencing PTSD and anxiety due to my birth and postpartum experiences, and since I had a newborn, rest was nonexistent. I wasn't my usual silly, joke-telling self. I was angry and snappy. I cried often. My husband noticed and took the baby so that I could go do something for myself. I initially felt silly when he said that, because I was so deep in my own fog that I didn't know what to do for myself. I had forgotten what made me happy. I took a moment to think about it, and I made a list.

"My happy list" became my toolbox for whenever I needed a break and to recharge. Sometimes it was a spa day. Most times it was a trip to Target to buy a bunch of candles and things I didn't need. One of my favorite go-tos was to go for a drive while listening to my favorite podcast or music with the windows down. Fresh air and the nostalgia of 1990s and 2000s hip hop and R&B always put me in a good mood. I want you to do the same thing. You are just as important as the titles you hold, so you must take care of yourself.

Now, it's time to create your happy list. In the space below, write down a list of things—big or small, simple or complex—that make you happy. Keep this list somewhere easily accessible for you to always refer back to.

_____

_____

_____

_____

_____

_____

_____

_____

_____

_____

_____

_____

TIME STEAL ZONE (TSZ)

There will be seasons when life gets busy, projects are due, and you simply need more hours in the day. Those hours are what I call time steal zones (TSZ). These are the hours of the day that can be used, if need be, for busy seasons, but aren't sustainable to use consistently as work hours. TSZs are usually in the early morning or late at night. For example, right now I am using my TSZ to complete this manuscript. We are in a busy season in my business, so I have a lot to do during the day and am not able to focus and concentrate the way I need to get this book done. I'm using the hours of five to seven in the morning to wake up and get it done. After my work is done, I pick up on my morning routine by praying and mindfully drinking my coffee. This works for me because I am a morning person, but if you are a night owl, you may find it helpful to stay up late to get work done. So that means your TSZ may be late into the night. It's important to remember that this zone is not for long-term use. If you work late into the night or wake up early in the morning, you're cutting into your rest and routines, and that is not healthy in the long run.

Rewrite your priorities below and, to the right of them, list how you're going to protect them when creating your schedule:

_____

_____

_____

_____

_____

At this point, you now have your goals, priorities, hats, and time found that we can allocate to more productive activities. We've also covered the importance of rest and having a routine. With all of that in mind, it's time to create the layout of your schedule. When adding things to your schedule, do them in this order:

1. Add your fixed activities. These are the things that don't change and you have minimal control over, such as work, school, drop-offs/pick-ups, etc.
2. Your priorities and their prospective boundaries
3. Rest
4. Routines (AM/PM)

On the next page is an example of how that all comes together for me in a general blueprint. All my priorities are present: time with God (in my AM routine), my family (weekends and blocked out time during the week), my physical health (daily workout), and rest (in bed by nine p.m.). If I ever need more time, I can take it from my TSZ, or we can order out for dinner and I take the time from there. Again, that's not for a long-term plan though, just as needed.

	MONDAY	TUESDAY	WEDNESDAY	THURSDAY	FRIDAY	SATURDAY	SUNDAY
5:00 a.m. - 6:00 a.m.	TSZ	TSZ	TSZ	TSZ	TSZ		
6:00 a.m. - 7:00 a.m.	AM Routine	AM Routine	AM Routine	AM Routine	AM Routine		
7:00 a.m. - 8:30 a.m.	Mommy Mode	Mommy Mode	Mommy Mode	Mommy Mode	Mommy Mode		
9:00 a.m. - 10:00 a.m.	Workout	Workout	Workout	Workout	Workout		
10:30 a.m. - 11:00 a.m.	Get Dressed for the day	Get Dressed for the day	Get Dressed for the day	Get Dressed for the day	Get Dressed for the day	Boundary: No work on weekends. Family time only.	
11:00 a.m. - 4:30 p.m.	Work	Work	Work	Work	Work		
4:30 p.m.- 5:30 p.m.	Make Dinner	Make Dinner	Make Dinner	Make Dinner	Make Dinner		
5:30 p.m. - 7:00 p.m.	Family Time	Family Time	Family Time	Family Time	Family Time		
7:00 p.m. - 8:00 p.m.	Prepare for next day	Prepare for next day	Prepare for next day	Prepare for next day/Order Groceries	Prepare for next week		
8:00 p.m. - 9:00 p.m.	PM Routine	PM Routine	PM Routine	PM Routine	PM Routine		

Your turn! Use the blank template on the next page to create the general blueprint for your life. This is 100 percent customizable for you. You may need to work on the weekends. You may need to go to bed later. You may work longer. Whatever the situation is, it's okay. Just create the plan and don't forget to include:

1. Your fixed activities
2. Your priorities and their prospective boundaries
3. Rest
5. Routines (AM/PM)

TIME	MONDAY	TUESDAY	WEDNESDAY	THURSDAY	FRIDAY	SATURDAY	SUNDAY

Congratulations! Are you excited? You should be. You've just created a structure for your total life success. This is the foundation of what your week will look like in order to operate as efficiently as possible in every area of your life.

PHASE 3: EXECUTE

This is the phase that goes beyond this book. It's now time for you to take this plan you've crafted and do it. As you begin to implement this new schedule, I want you to keep in mind the following: the focused five, plan before you land, and weekly self-evaluations.

THE FOCUSED FIVE

I've made the mistake many times of putting too much on my to-do list to complete in a day. I end up finishing the day either feeling really accomplished and burnt out or beating myself up because there's so much that I didn't get done. The reason I had you document how long it takes you to do things is because you need to know how long it takes you to do something in order to properly plan to do it. If you have a to-do list of ten things to get done in a day, the list may not look long. But if each thing takes two hours to complete, that's not realistic. This is why I created the concept of the focused five. This means that your to-do list should not exceed five tasks that you can completely zero in on to get done in a day. You enforce the focused aspect of this time by putting your phone on do not disturb, turning off notifications on your computer, or going to a quiet place and working uninterrupted. With this concept, you're able to make your workload realistic and be a lot more productive with your day.

PLAN BEFORE YOU LAND

One of the biggest time-wasters of a day is thinking about what you have to do. Have you been there? Waking up to start your day and looking at your calendar, planner, or master to-do list and thinking about where you need to start. Doing this is once again starting your day in a reactive way and not proactive. The concept of plan before you land means to plan out your days before they start. This way, you wake up and know exactly what you need to do. No thinking is involved. You can do this the evening before, or you can do this further in advance. I like to plan out my next week on Fridays. I look at everything I have going on personally and in my business, and I plan my focused five for each day of the following week. Choose a day that fits best within your blueprint and plan before you land.

WEEKLY SELF-EVALUATIONS

I believe that self-awareness is the secret to success. Having a check-in every week allows you to remove yourself from the grind and check in with your own well-being and objectively evaluate your productivity. In chapter two, I told you about a breakdown I had in a moment of being overwhelmed. After I finished crying out of frustration, I began to craft this concept of weekly self-evaluations. In that situation in particular, I wanted to check in with the root of my emotions in an effort to make the necessary changes. While doing that, I realized that I felt imbalanced because my business required so much of me in order to run and grow. That wasn't a big deal before, but now that I am a mother, I am not willing to give that much of myself to where I don't have much left for my family.

That revelation turned into me re-evaluating my business, implementing more passive income streams, and hiring more team members. I made it a goal that, when it comes to my business, I would only do the things that only I could do. I would need to delegate everything else. That decision shifted my company in a pivotal way. I now operate as the executive only, and it has given me the freedom of my time back without compromising my success. Seeing the result of that decision made me implement weekly self-evaluations as part of my blueprint, and I want you to do the same. An evaluation will allow you to course-correct before you get overwhelmed. It's important to note, though, that for this to work, you must possess the capacity to be objective and not self-deprecating. Self-awareness is not self-deprecating. If you aren't able to do that, this will do more harm than good. Go back to your blueprint and set aside time to do a weekly self-evaluation, and then implement your findings into how you go about your next week.

Here's what to ask yourself:

1. How am I really doing this week?
2. What did I do well this week?
3. Where did I miss the mark?
4. What can I do next week to improve upon where I missed the mark?

PHASE 4: ACCOUNTABILITY

The American Society of Training and Development (ASTD) did a study on accountability and found that you have a 65 percent chance of completing a goal if you commit to someone that you'll do it. And if you have a specific accountability appointment with a person to whom you've committed, you will increase your chance of success by up to 95 percent. This is why this phase is so important. I want you to find a like-minded person who is going to hold you accountable for implementing the plan you created and making the necessary changes to improve upon it as you continue to do it. Be sure that this person is also someone of faith, because you don't want them to influence you out of alignment with God. You want them to sharpen iron (Proverbs 27:17) and not corrupt good habits (1 Corinthians 15:33).

Use the space below to write down the names of some people you have in mind and when you're going to reach out to ask them to be your accountability partner.

_____

_____

_____

Friend, if you follow every step outlined in these four phases, you're on the way to mastering your life. It's important to know that the blueprint will change and adjust as you get into your efficiency flow, but this foundation is one that will set you up for success. As you go to implement what you've outlined, give yourself grace. Be nice to yourself, and give yourself room to get it wrong while course-correcting to get it right.

CONCLUSION

MARTHA VS. MARY

Luke 10:38-42—The Passion Translation

As Jesus and the disciples continued on their journey, they came to a village where a woman welcomed Jesus into her home. Her name was Martha and she had a sister named Mary. Mary sat down attentively before the Master, absorbing every revelation he shared. But Martha became exasperated with finishing the numerous household chores in preparation for her guests, so she interrupted Jesus and said, "Lord, don't you think it's unfair that my sister left me to do all the work by myself? You should tell her to get up and help me."

The Lord answered her, "Martha, my beloved Martha. Why are you upset and troubled, pulled away by all these many distractions? Mary has discovered the one thing most important by choosing to sit at my feet. She is undistracted, and I won't take this privilege from her."

Are you Martha or Mary? I would dare to say that when you first started reading this book, you identified more with Martha. Aware of the Lord's presence, letting Him in, but being so busy with what you have to get done that you miss the opportunity to be fully present and attentive to what He's saying in the moment. I pray that, at this point, you see the importance of Mary and having a clear allegiance to Christ as the first priority. Martha was a go-getter, she knew things in the kitchen needed to be done, so she did them. But Mary had enough wisdom to know that, when the Lord is present, everything can wait. Martha's work ethic has a place, and so does yours, but it has to be clearly subordinate to your place as a servant of God. That's why this blueprint chapter is last. For women like us, Marthas by nature, becoming systematized to increase our efficiency is what we can adapt to easily. But it's tapping into our inner Mary that's going to be the determining factor to our success.

ACKNOWLEDGMENTS

To my loving husband—again, thank you for your unwavering support and love. I don't know where I'd be without you, and I don't want to know.

Grandma—Miracle Mary—thank you for your prayers and always loving me. I know God because you knew Him for the both of us until I surrendered to getting to know Him myself. Your prayers continue to live through everything I do.

Tanya, God sent you to my life. I could write a whole new book on the impact you've made on me. Thank you for always praying for me, speaking life into me, holding me accountable, and cheering me on. Thank you for leading through example and showing me through your actions what living for God really looks like. I couldn't have gotten this book done without you.

Pastor Vee, Leonarda, and Twanda—thank you for praying for me and my business. You all have showered me with so much love and support. I cannot thank you enough.

The current Anchored Media Team: Jalysa, Kylia, Faith, Christian, Keara—thank you for the work that you do to make me look good and make my dream such a sweet reality every day.

To the Mascot/Amplify publishing team, thank you for believing in me and the message I wanted to get across in this book.

To the listeners and supporters of *Blessed + Bossed Up* over the years, THANK YOU! THANK YOU! THANK YOU! I don't take for granted that you let me into your lives via my platform, and I pray that something that I've said has pushed you deeper in your relationship with Christ.